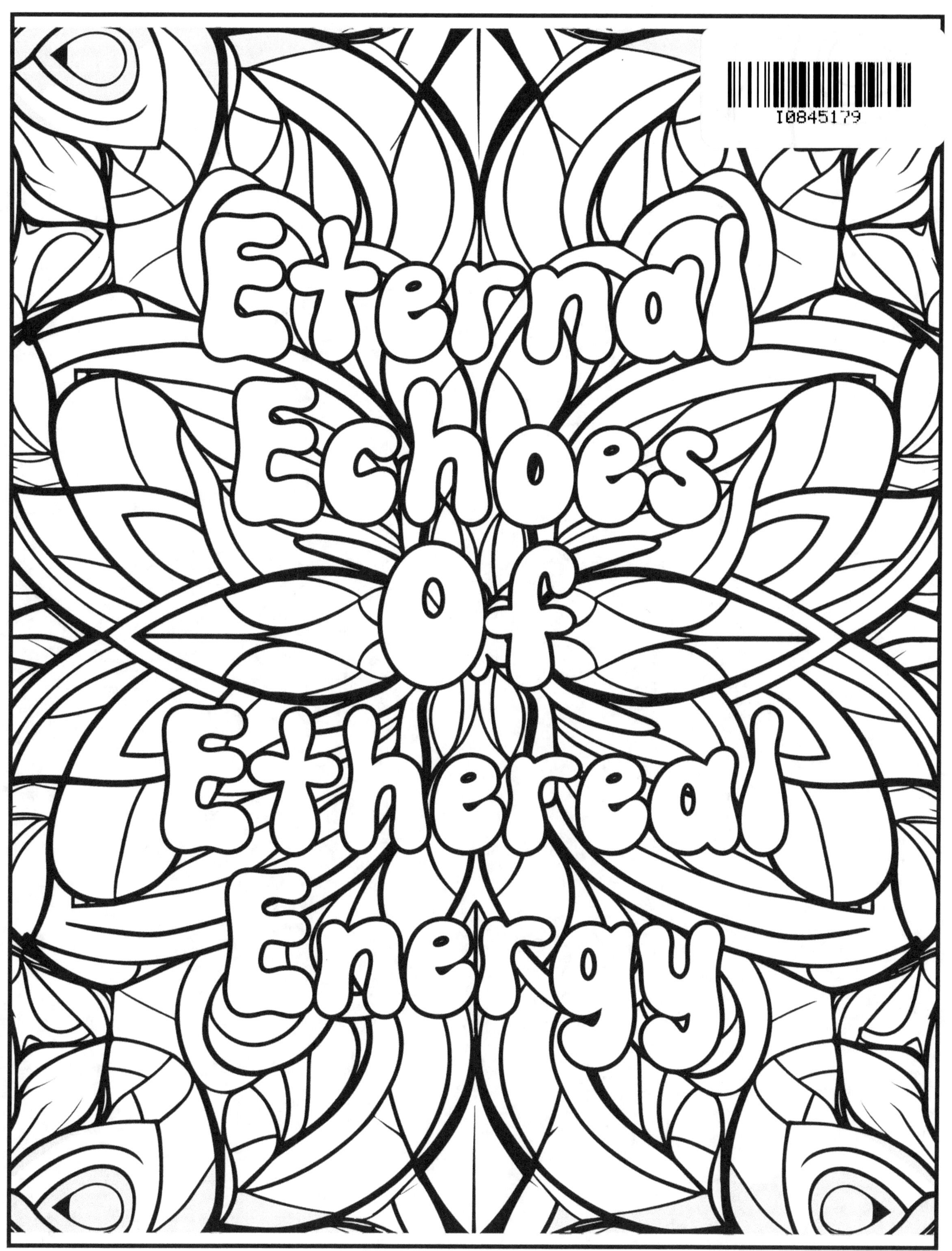

Eternal
Echoes
Of
Ethereal
Energy

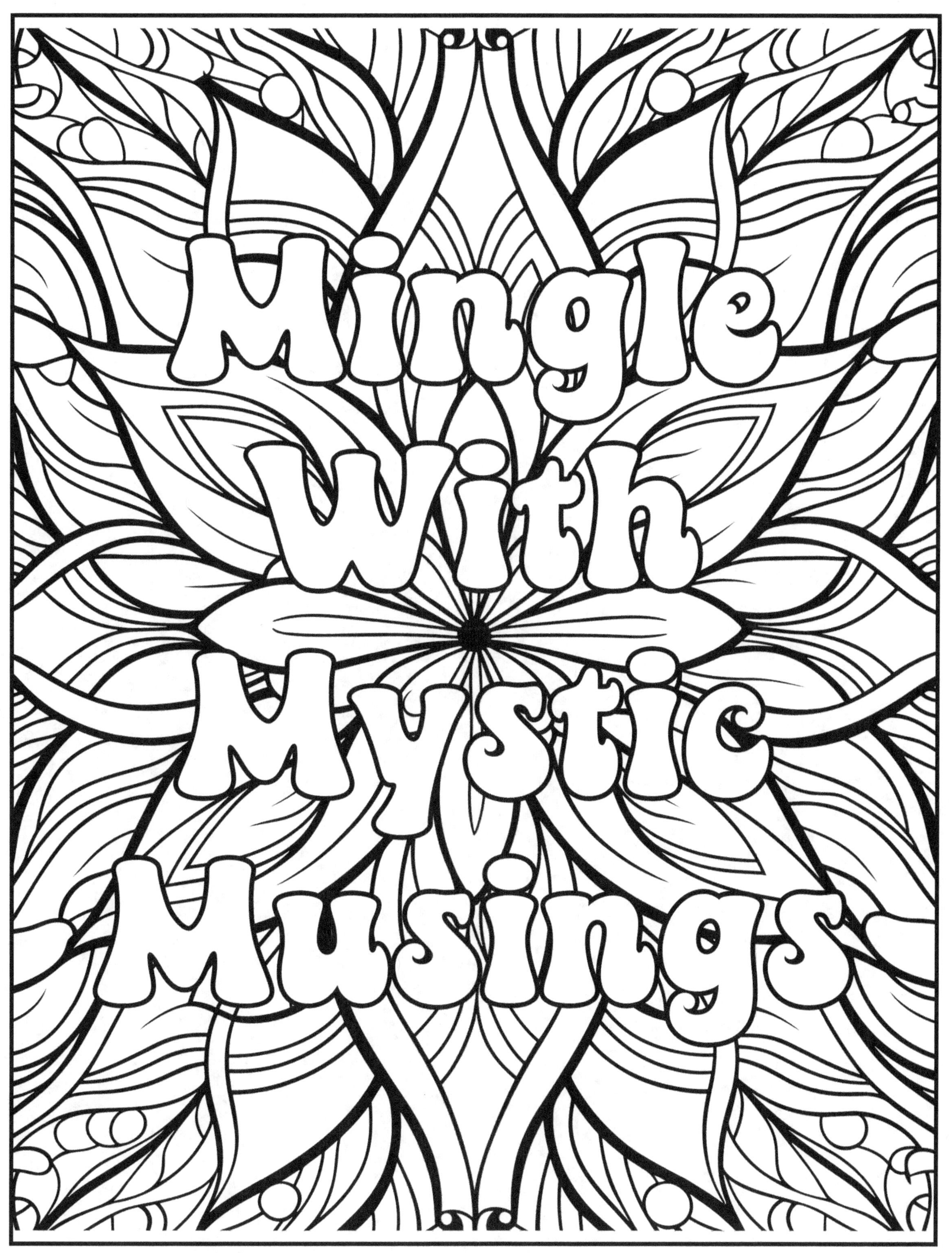

Mingle
With
Mystic
Musings

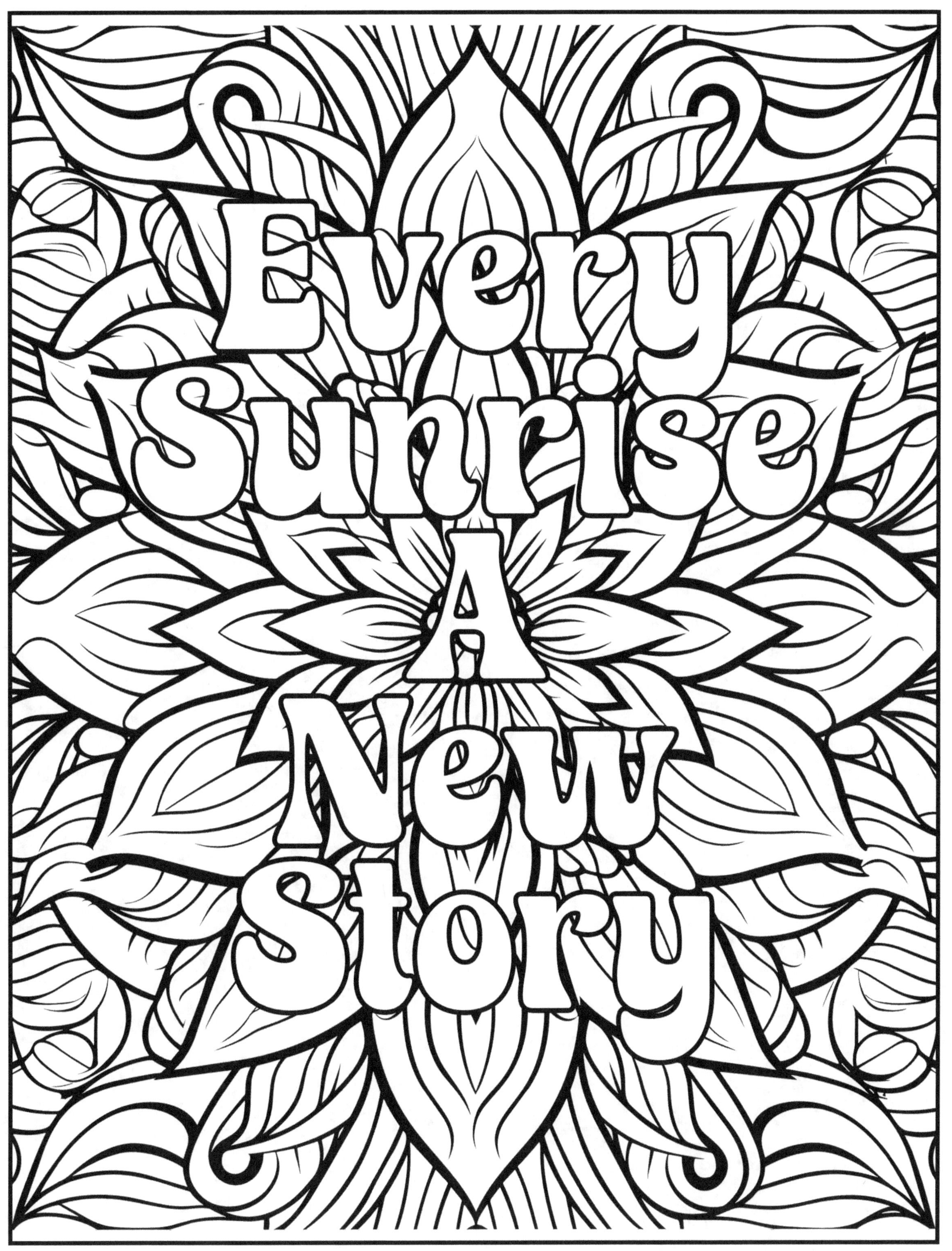
Every
Sunrise
A
New
Story

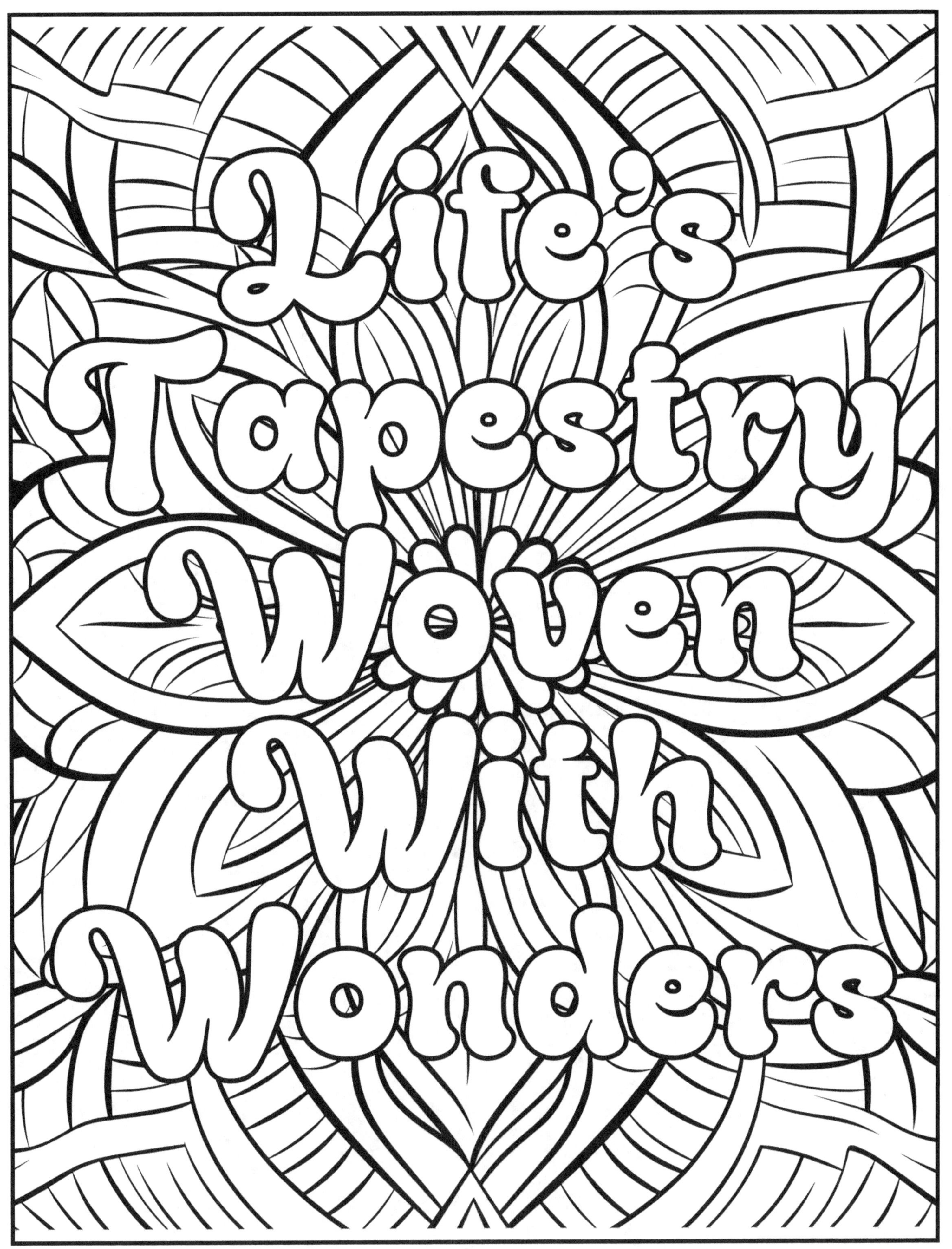

Life's
Tapestry
Woven
With
Wonders

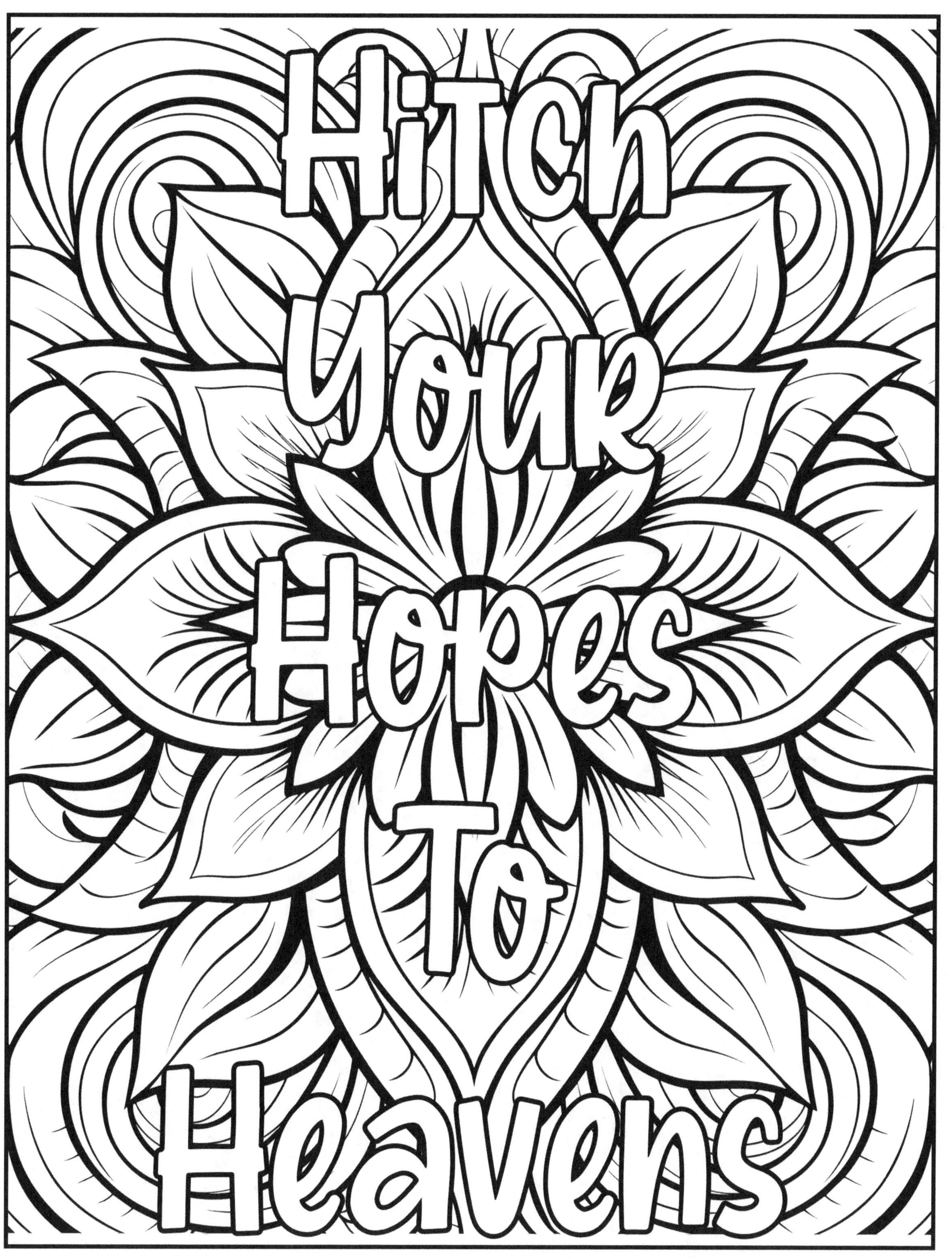

Hitch
Your
Hopes
To
Heavens

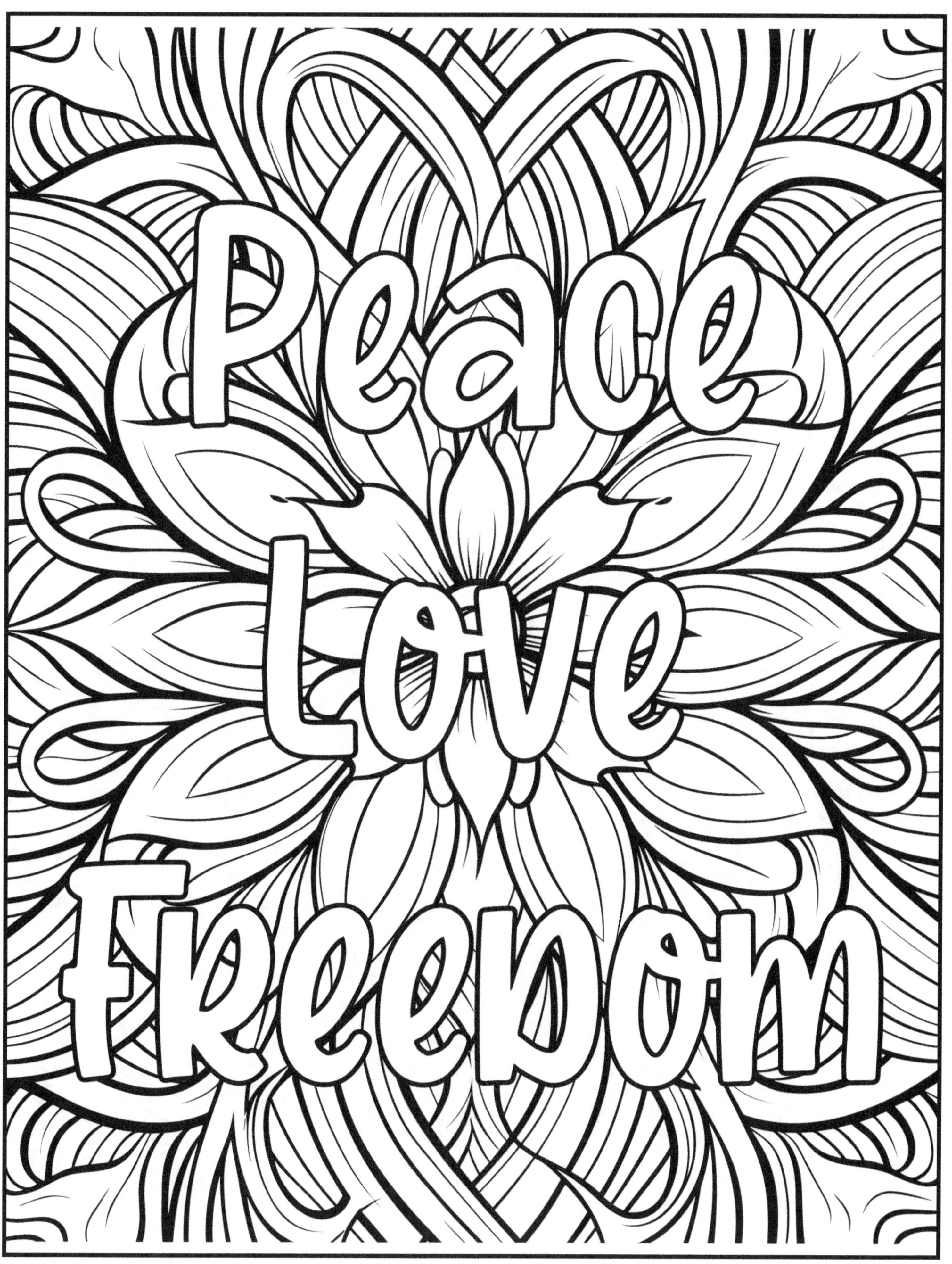
Peace
Love
Freedom

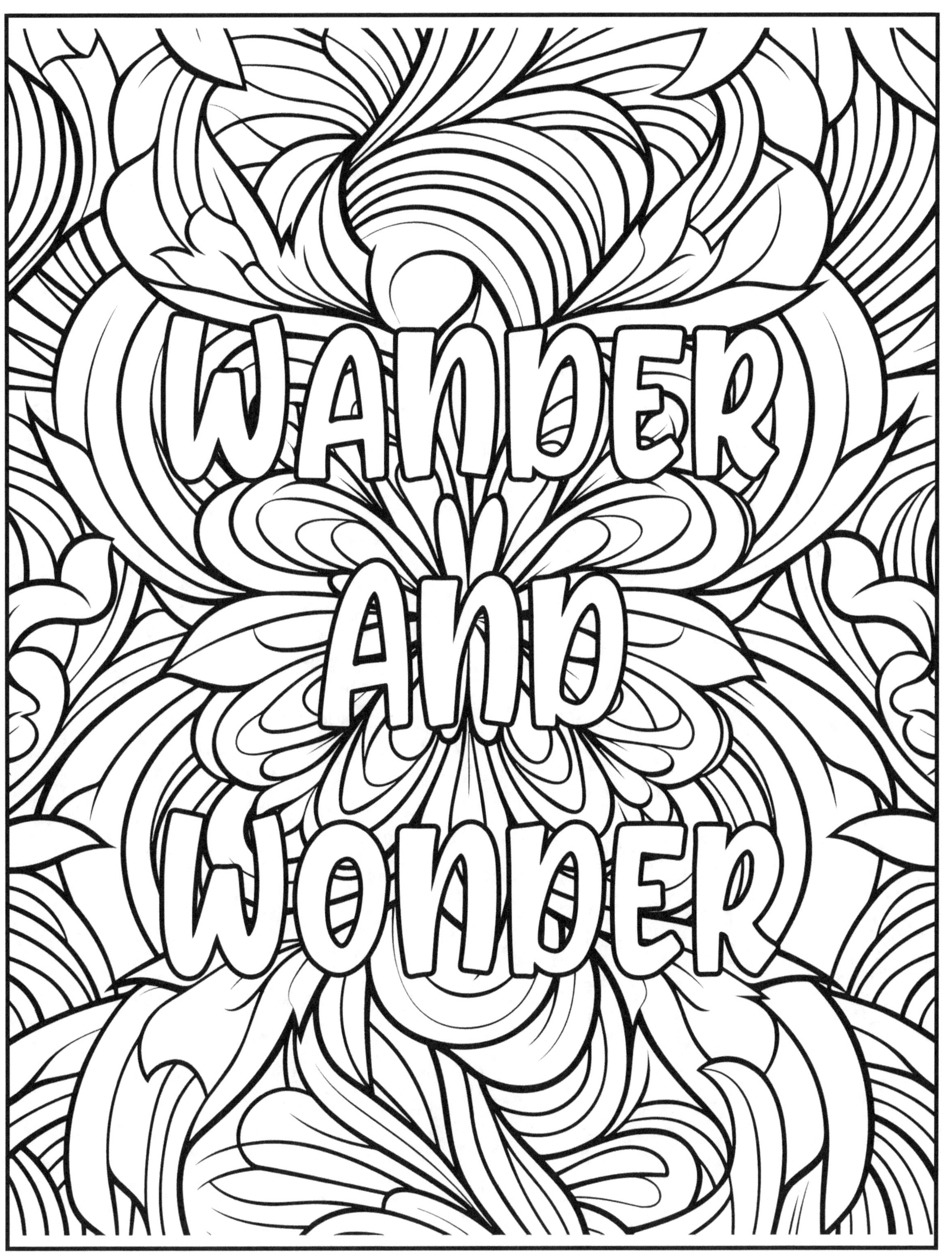

WANDER
AND
WONDER

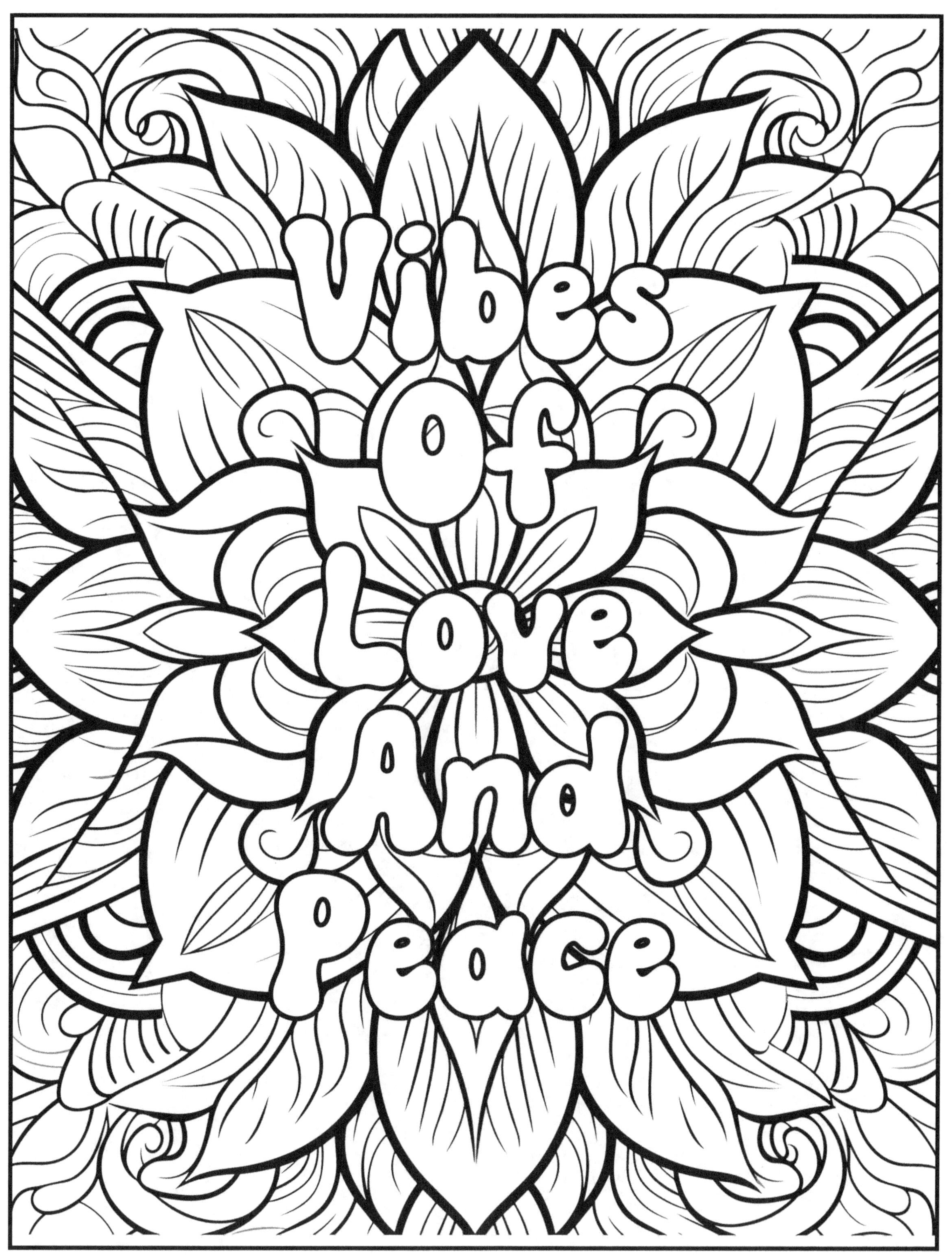

Vibes
Of
Love
And
Peace

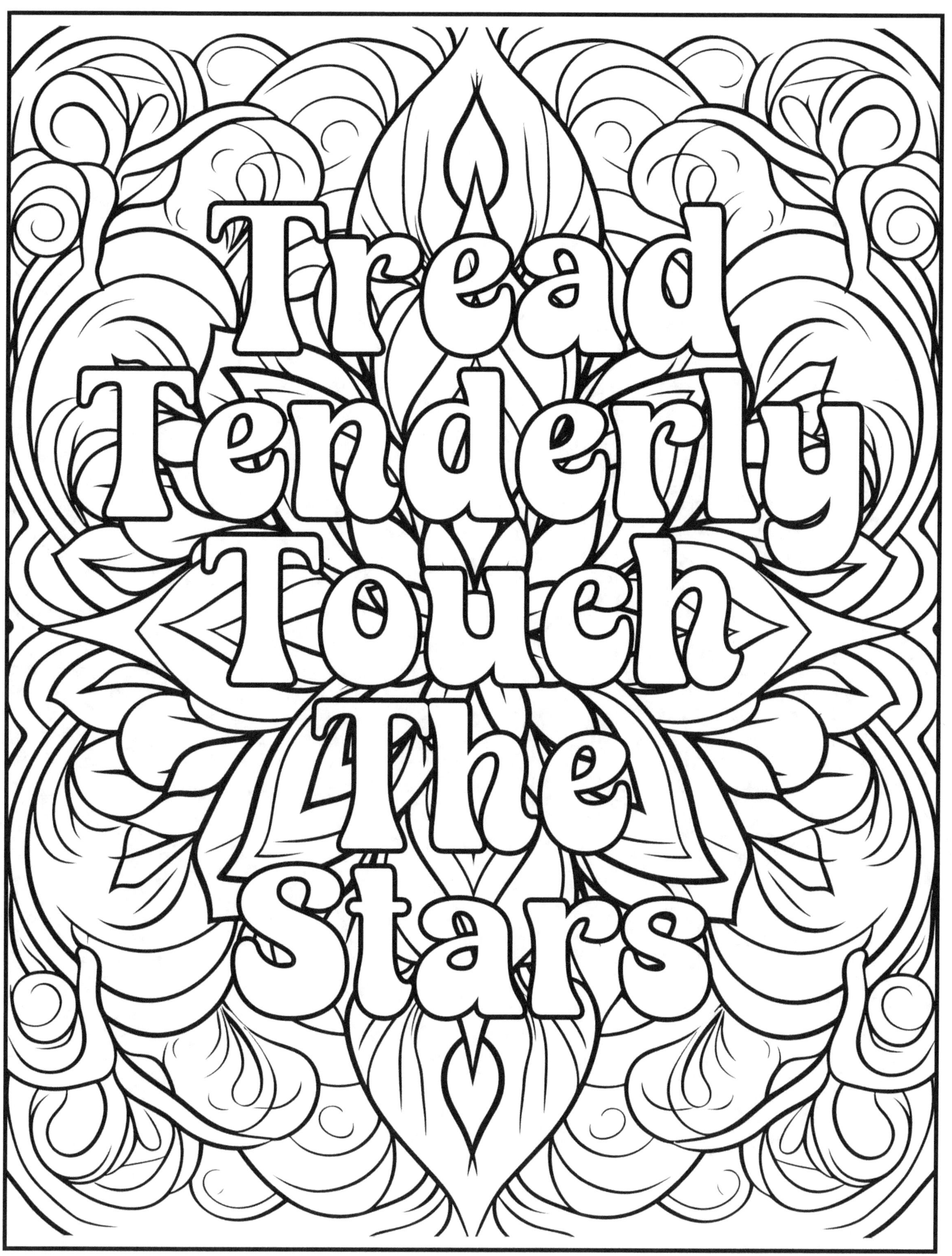

Tread
Tenderly
Touch
The
Stars

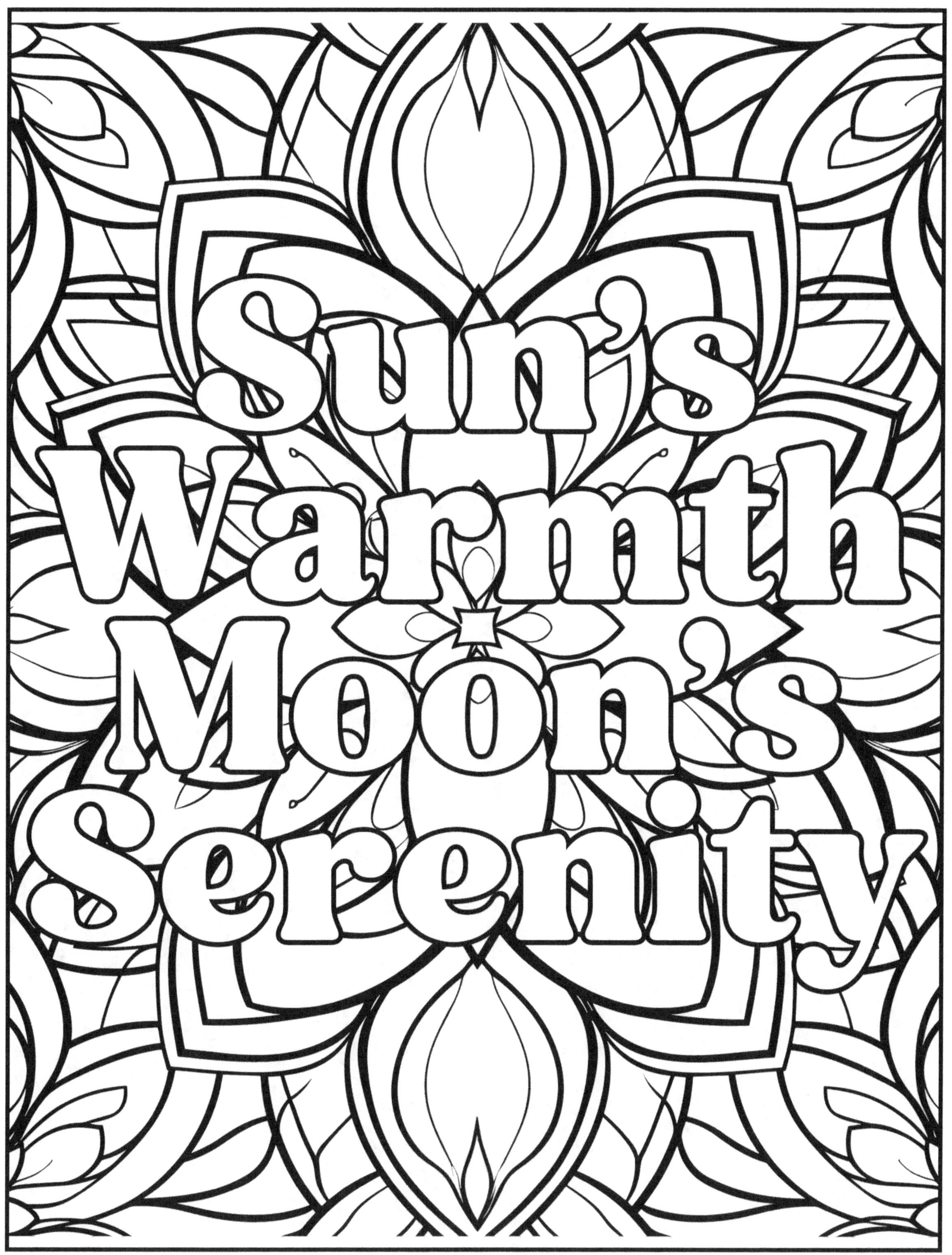

Sun's
Warmth
Moon's
Serenity

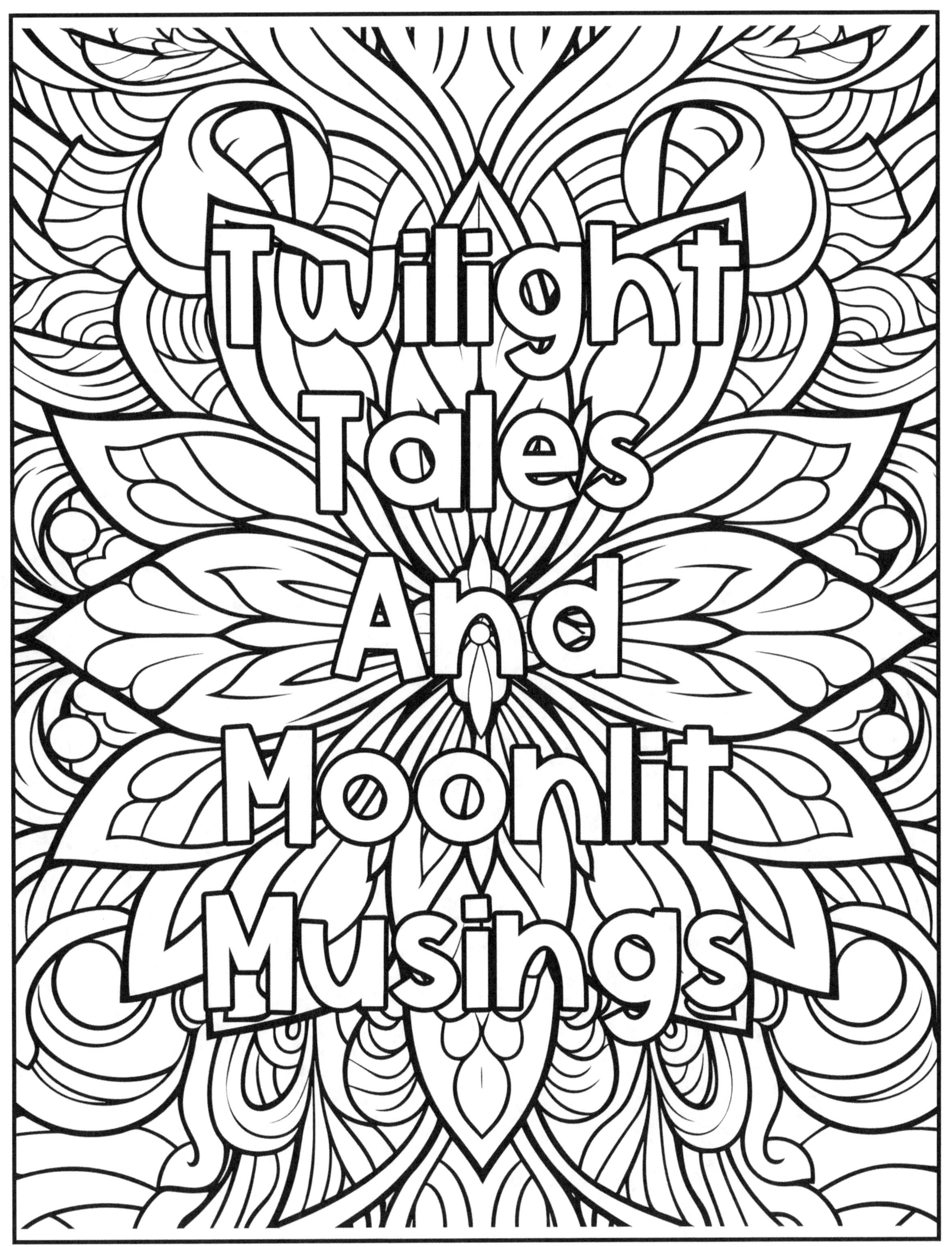

Twilight Tales And Moonlit Musings

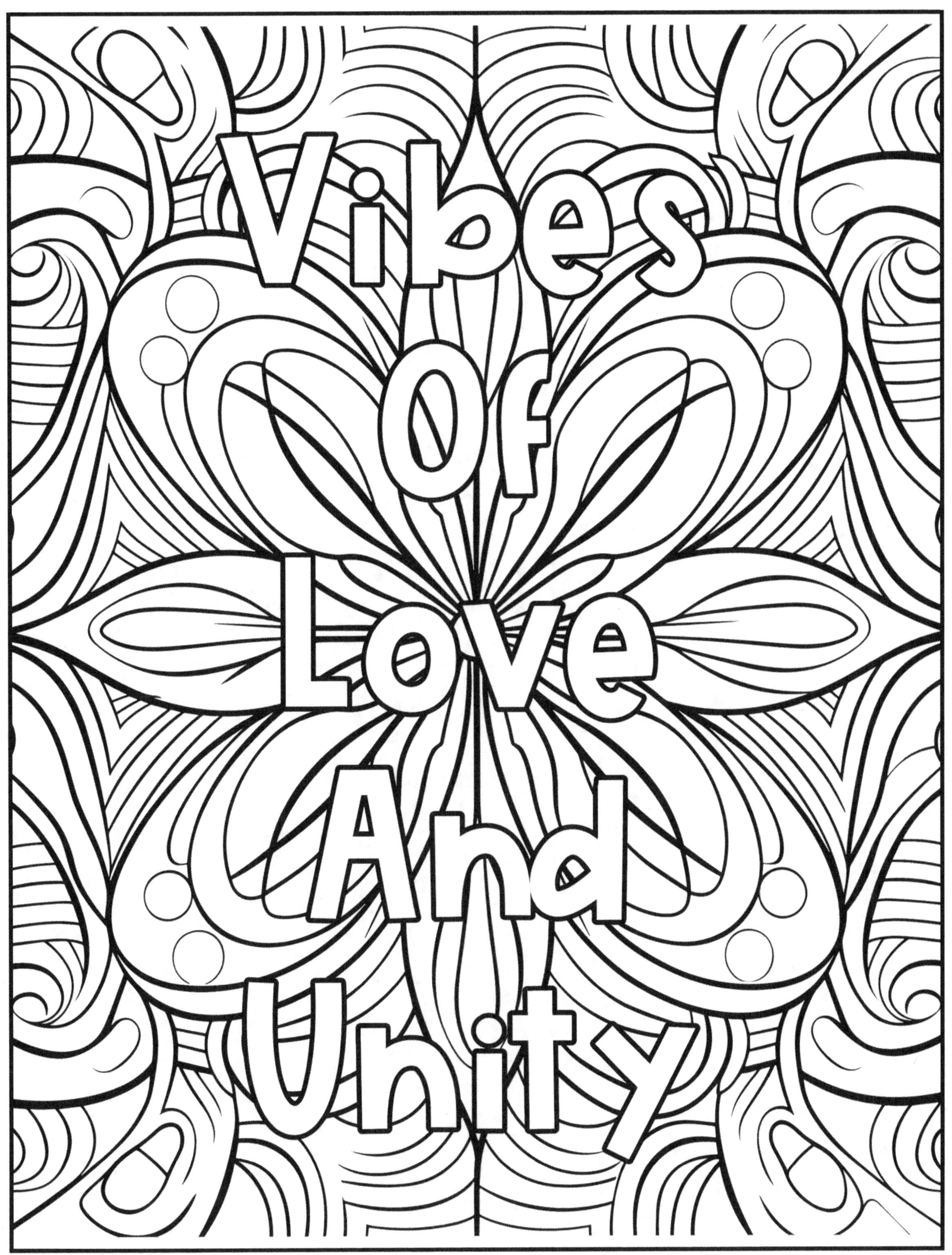

Vibes
Of
Love
And
Unity

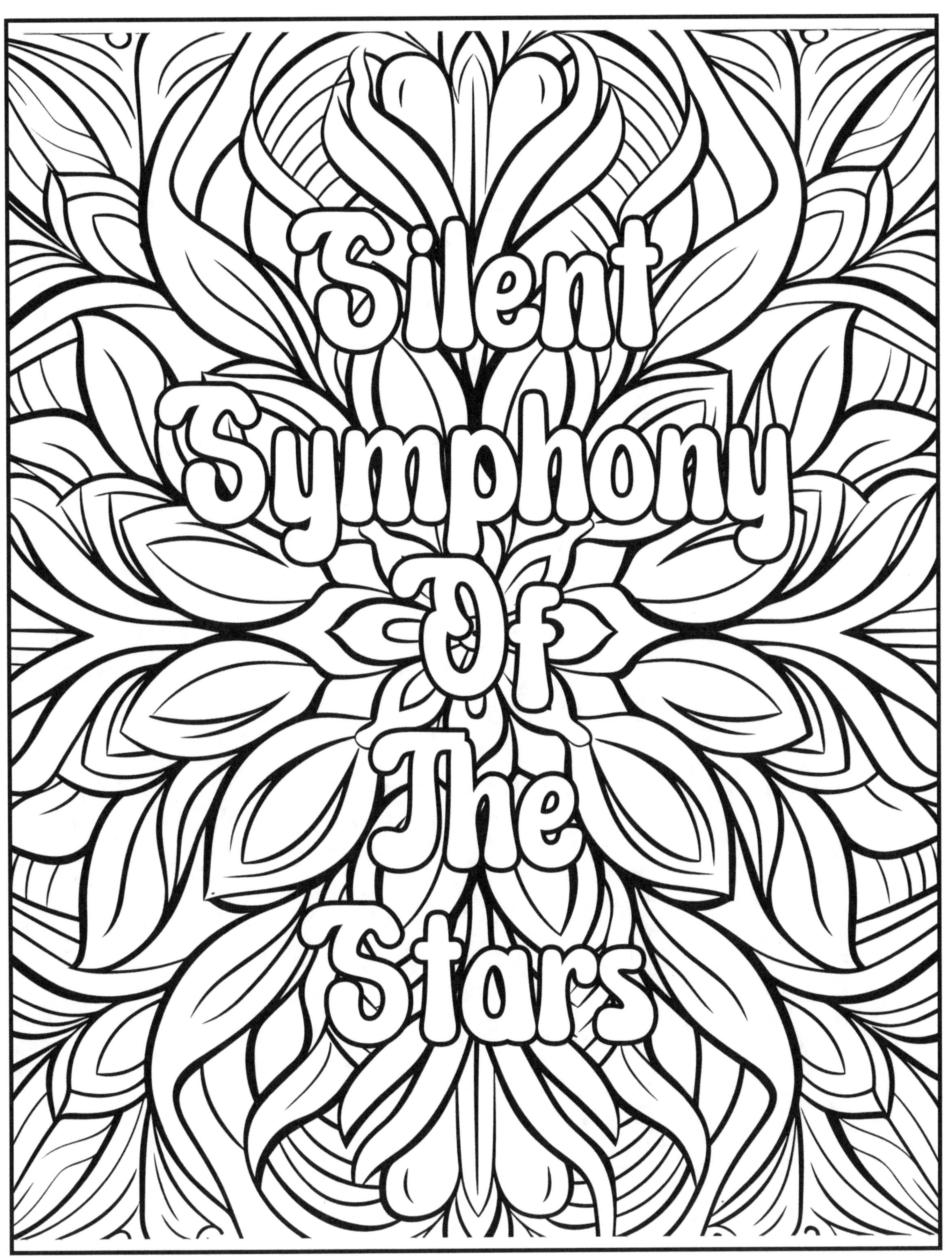

Silent
Symphony
Of
The
Stars

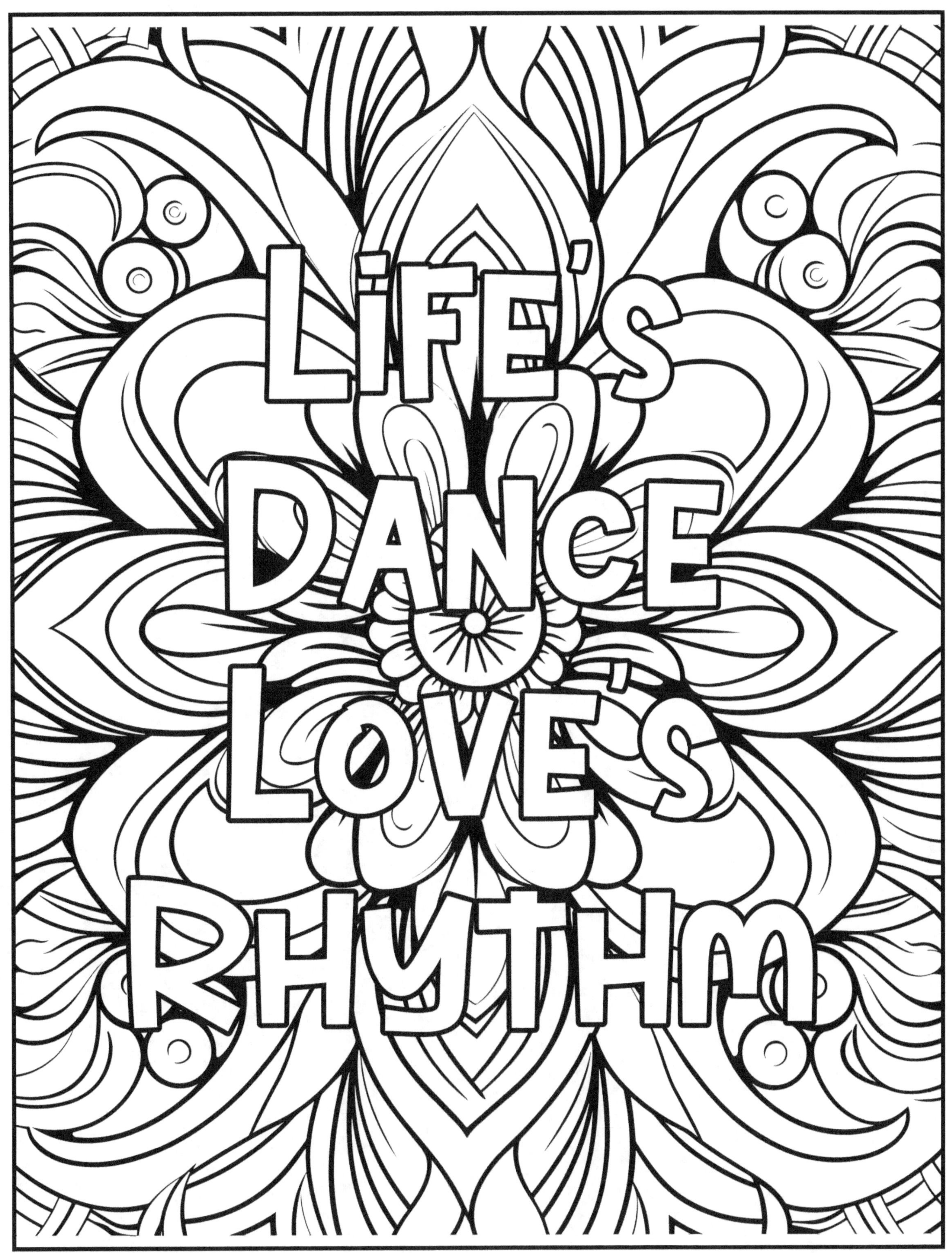

LIFE'S
DANCE
LOVE'S
RHYTHM

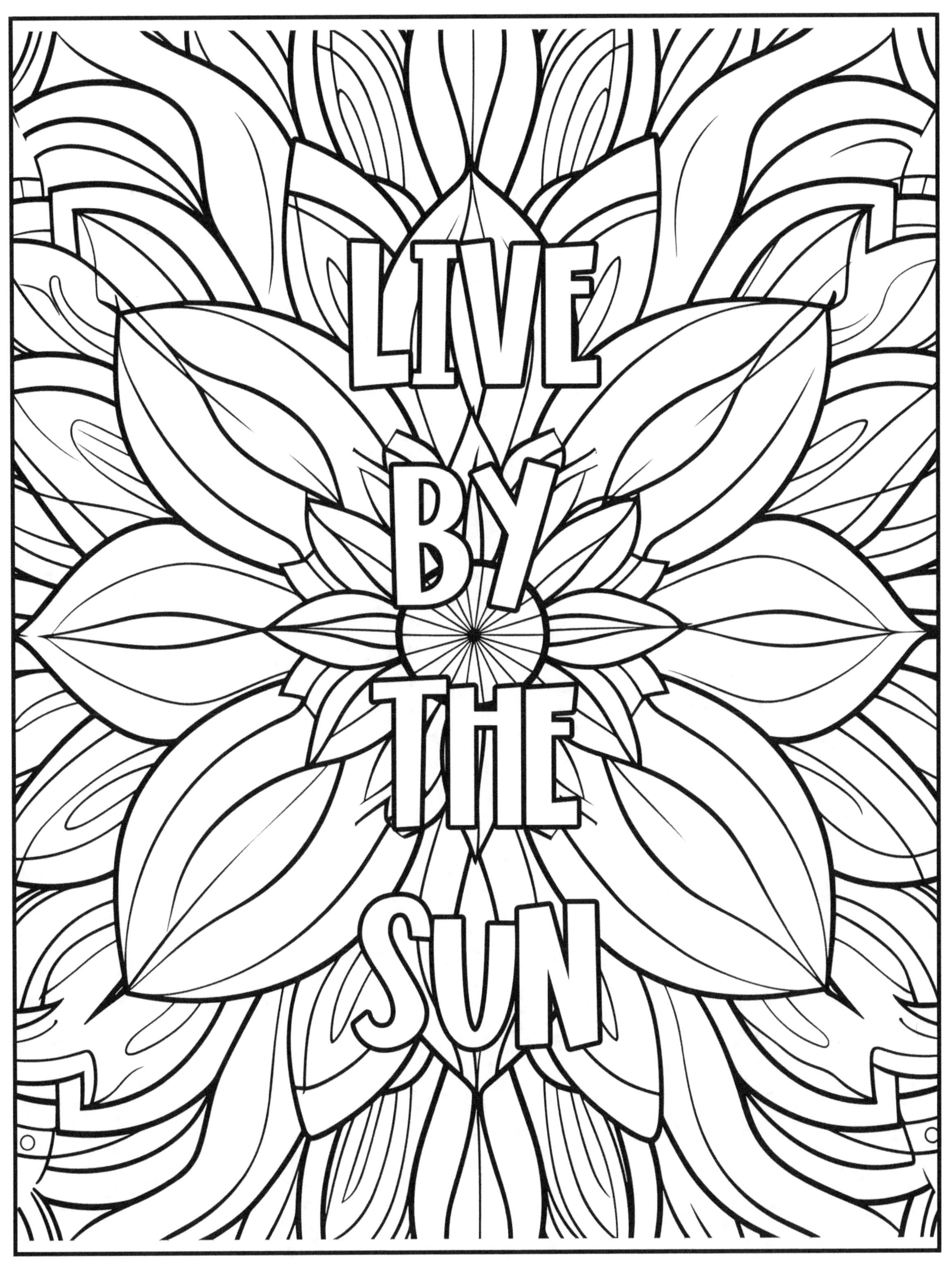

LIVE
BY
THE
SUN

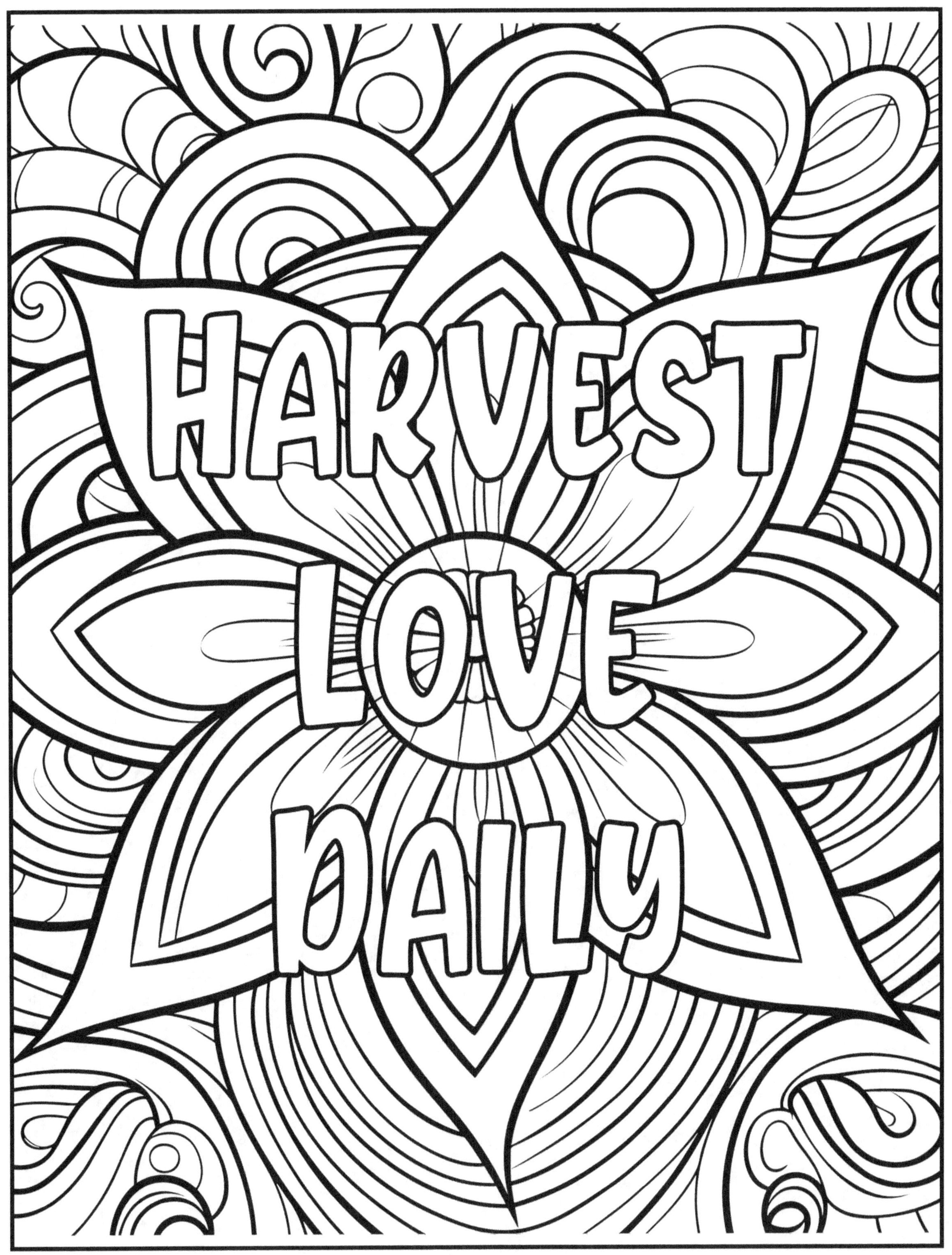

HARVEST
LOVE
DAILY

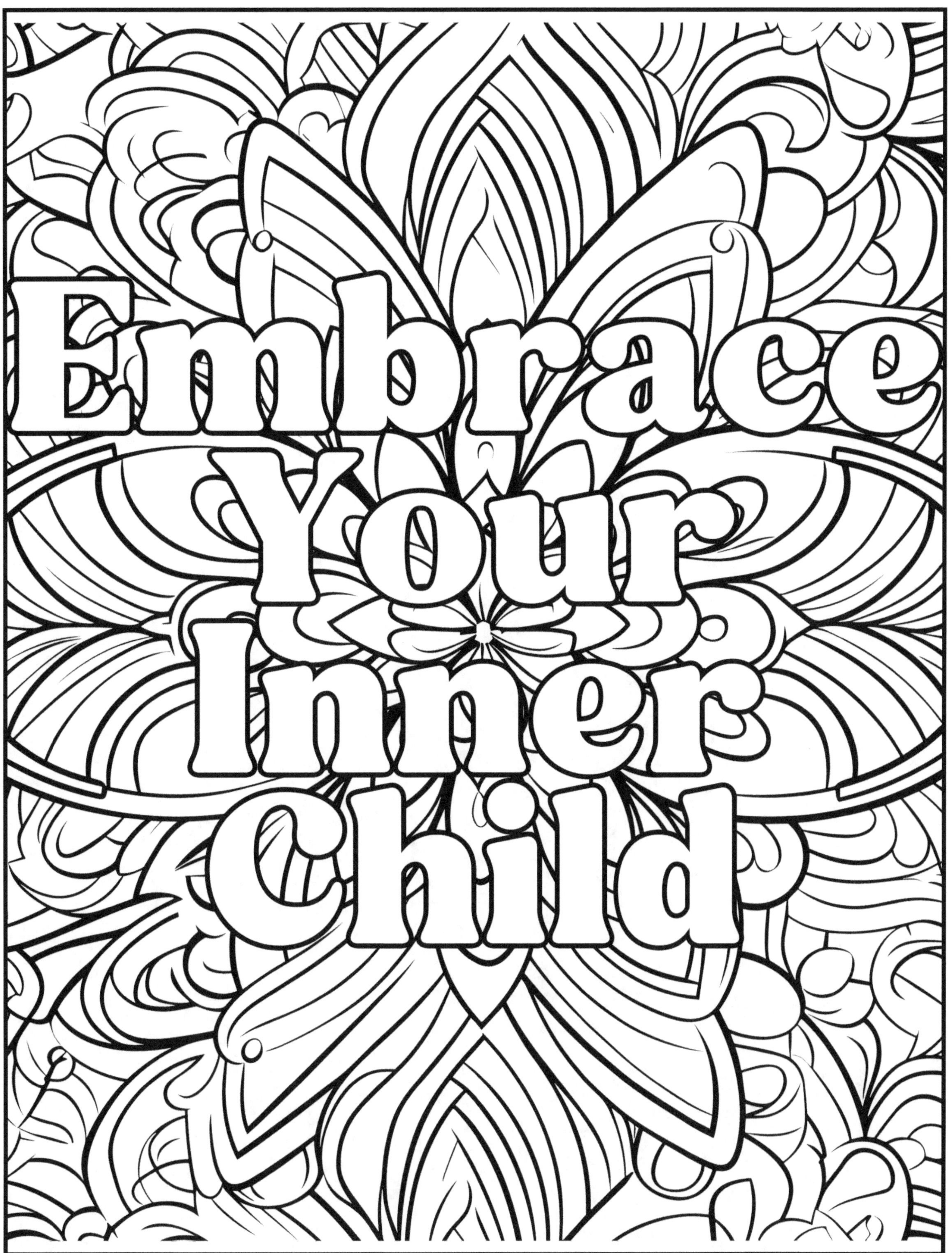

Embrace
Your
Inner
Child

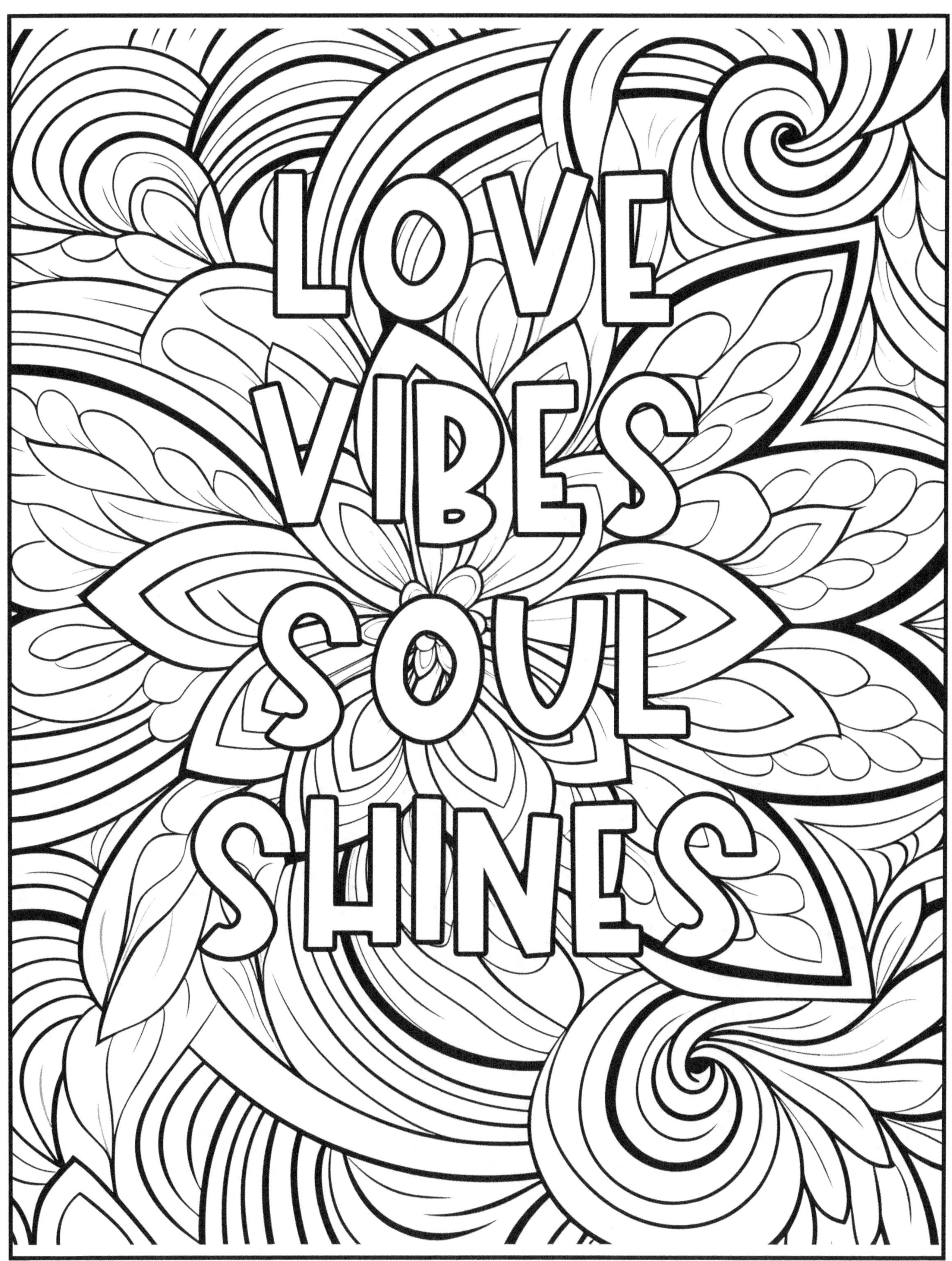

LOVE
VIBES
SOUL
SHINES

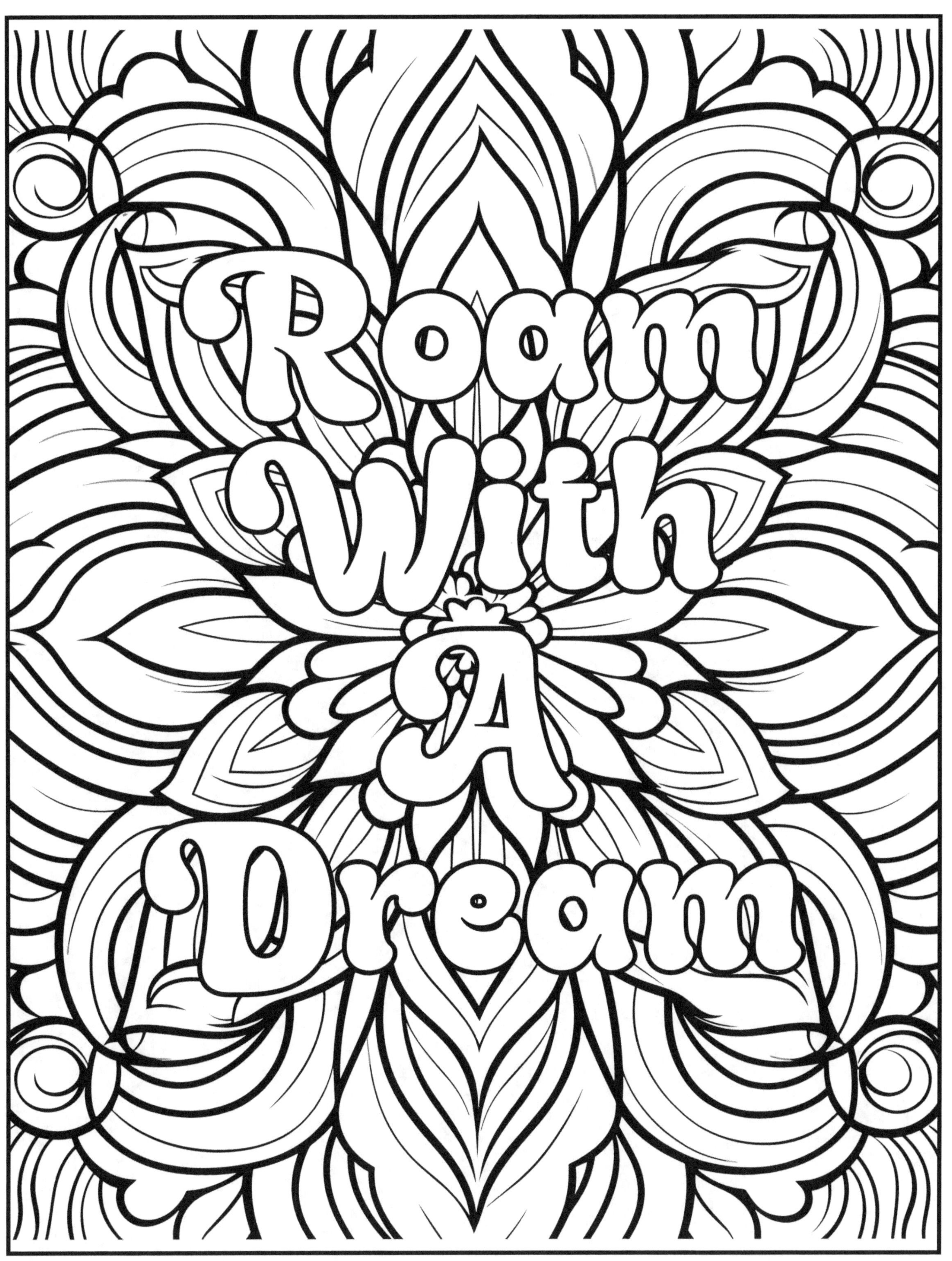

Roam
With
A
Dream

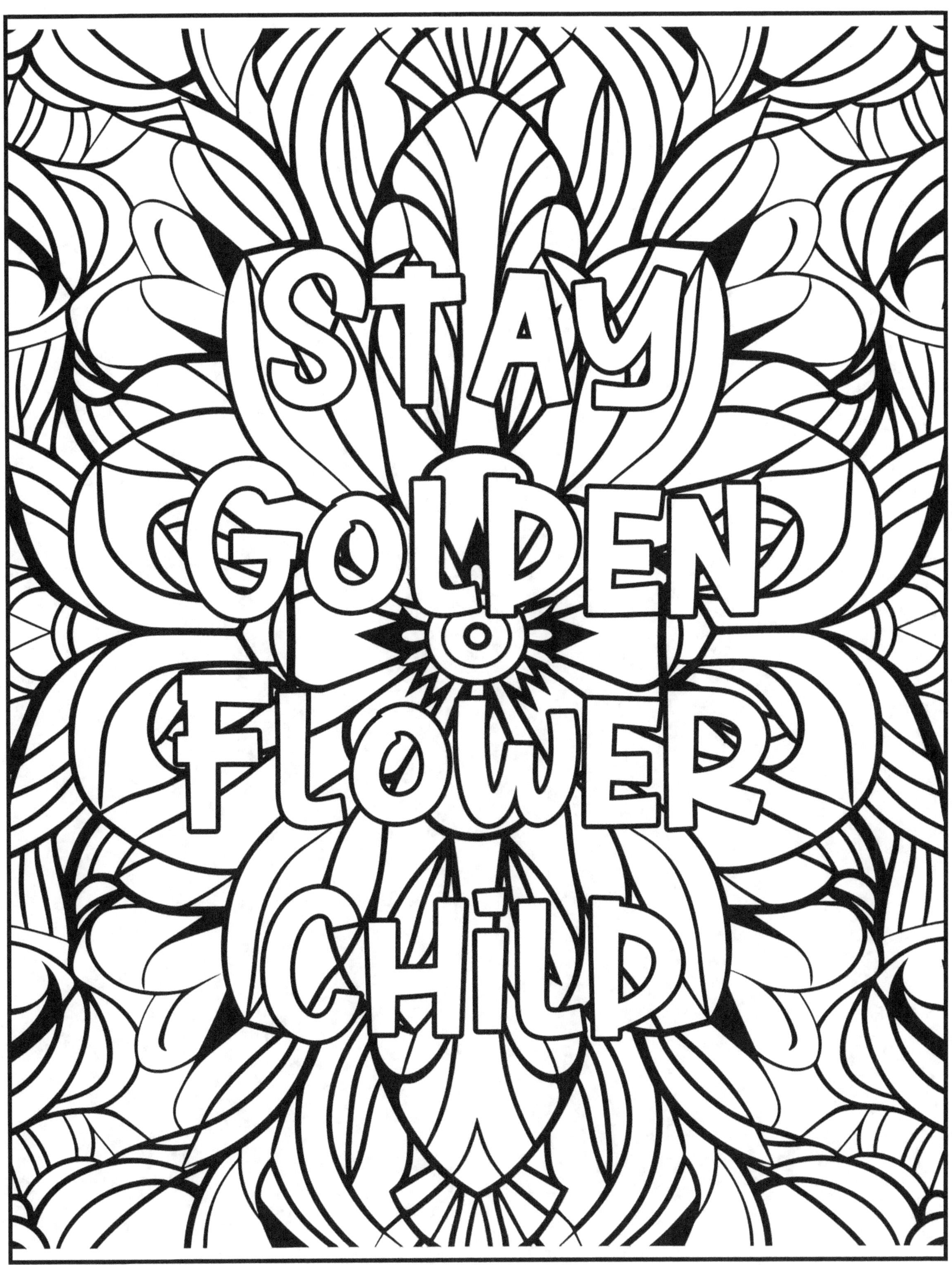

Stay
Golden
Flower
Child

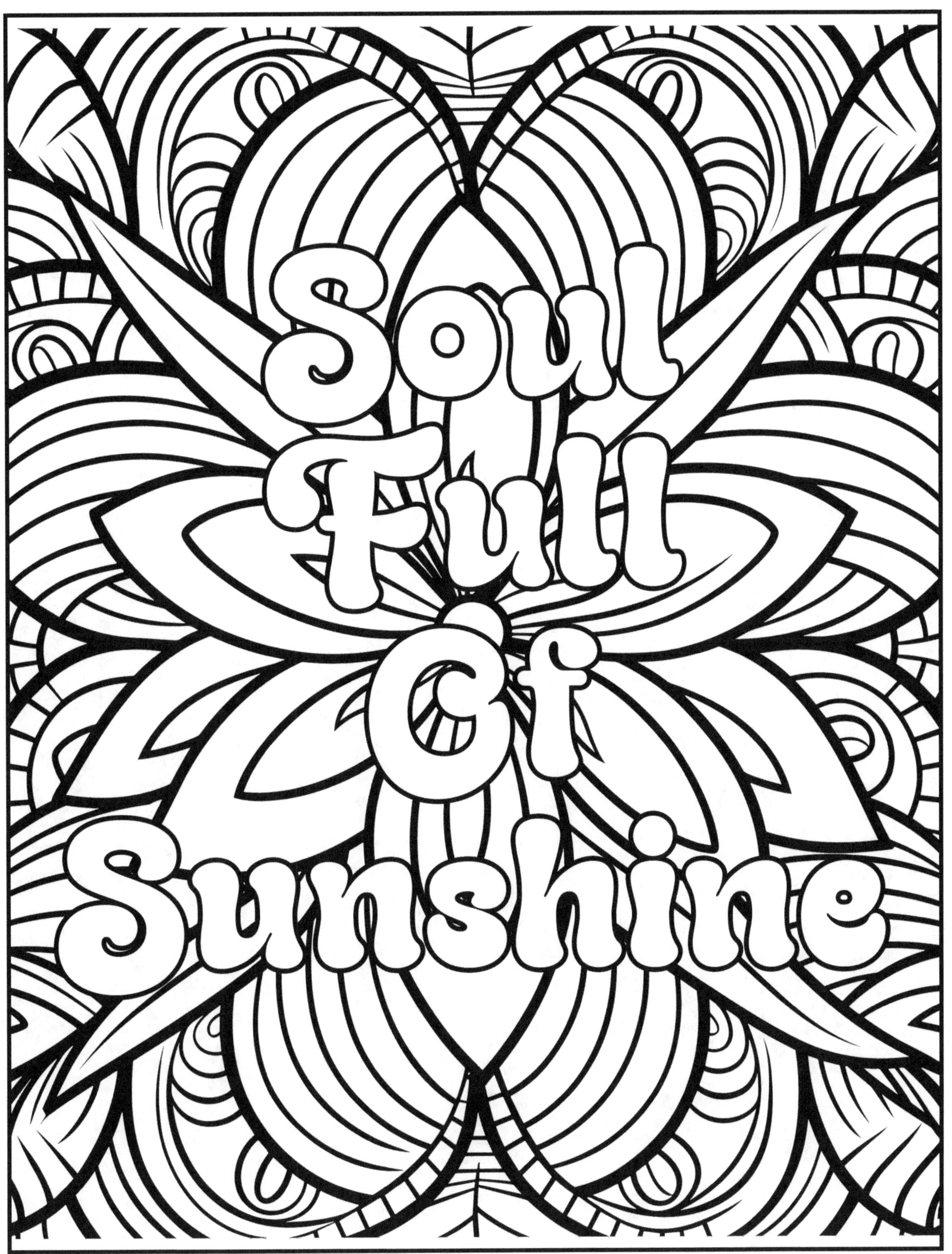

Soul
Full
Of
Sunshine

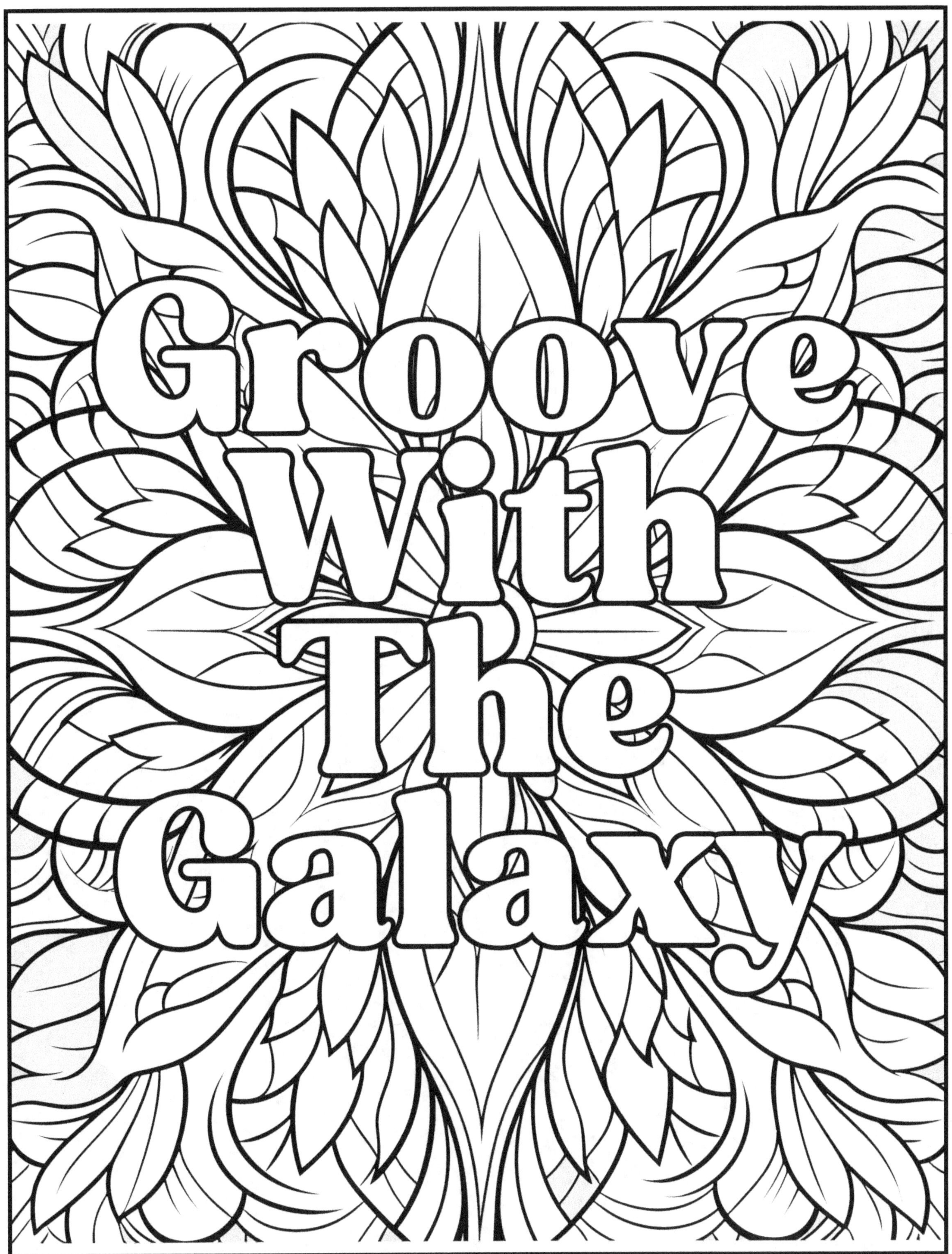

Groove
With
The
Galaxy

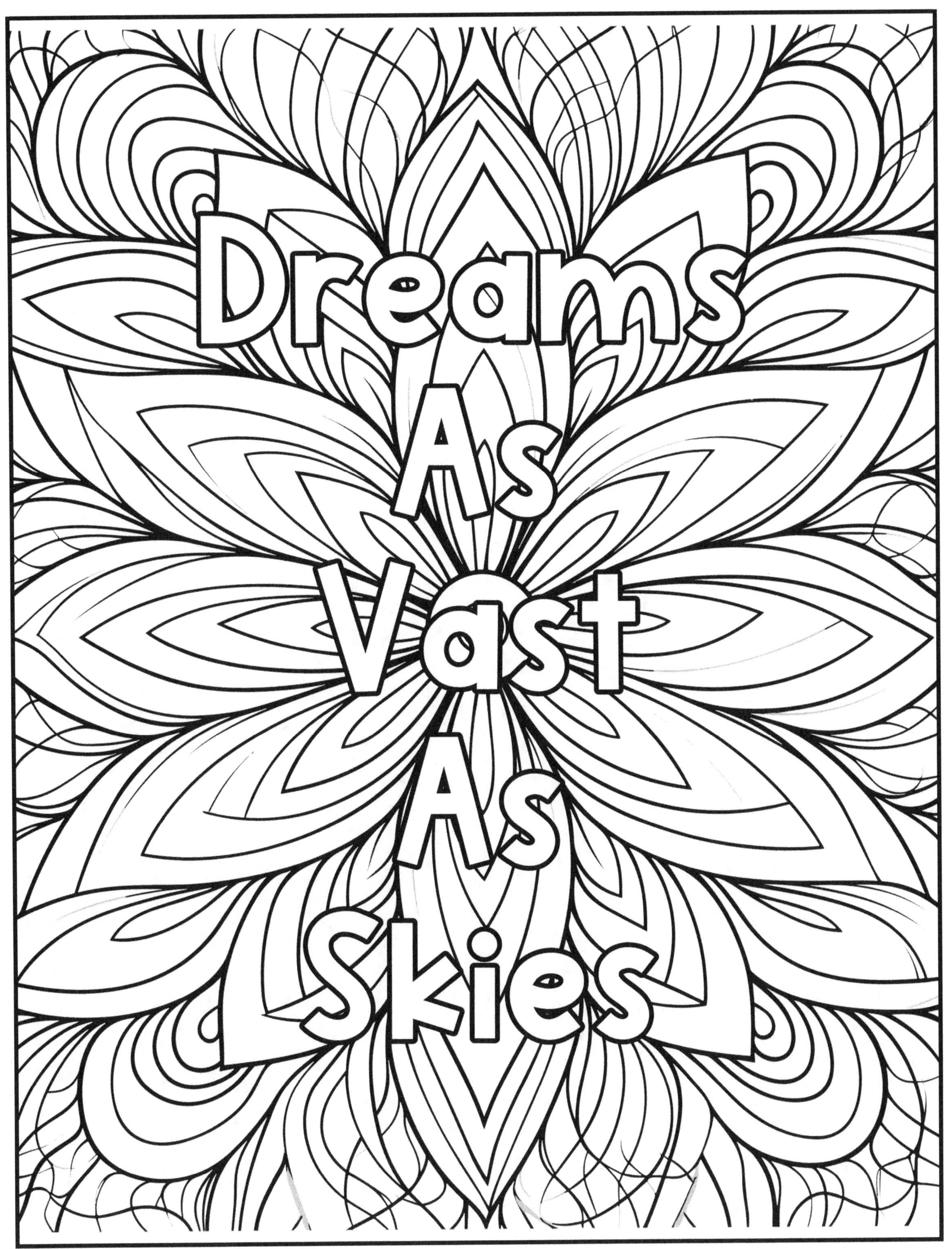

Dreams
As
Vast
As
Skies

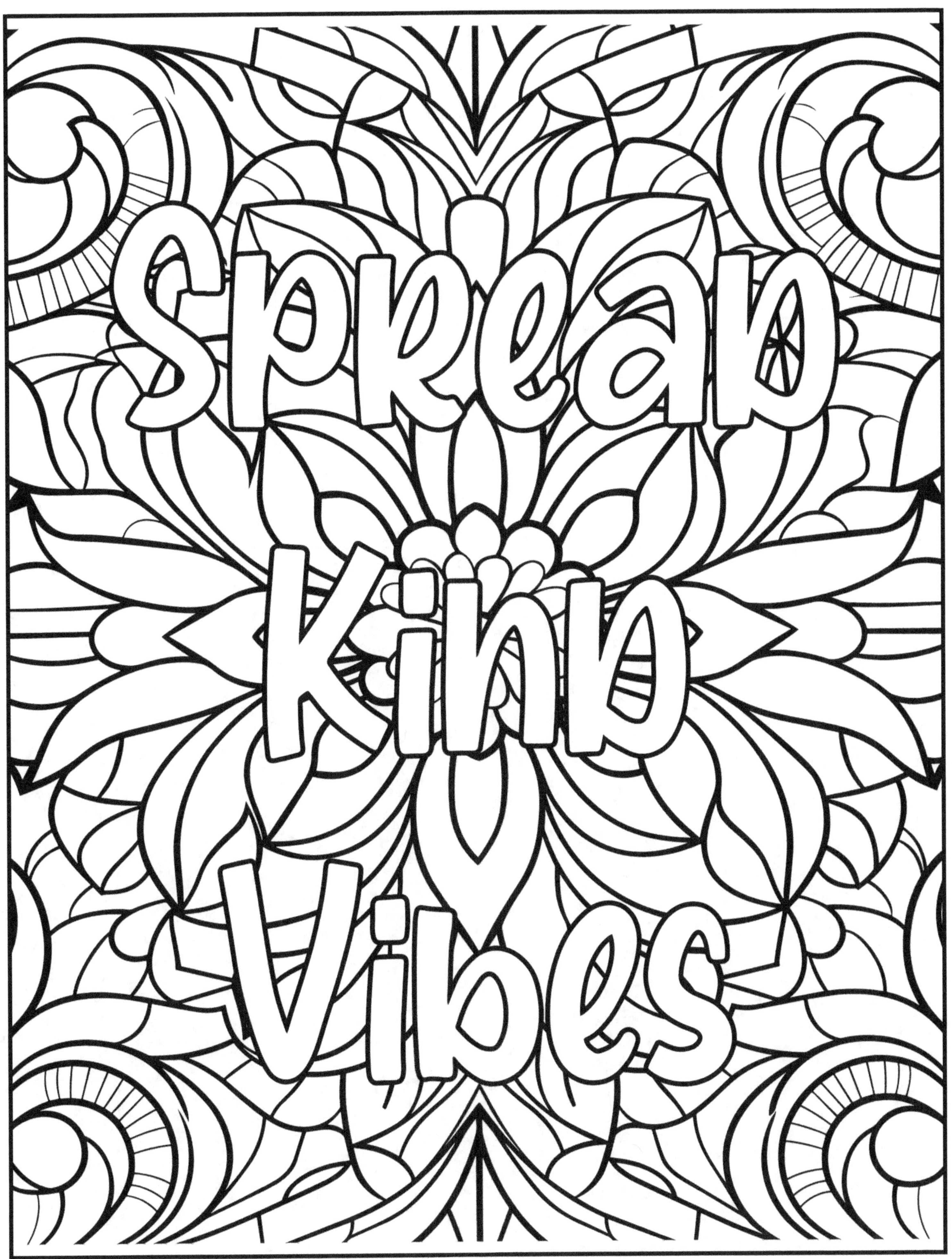

Spread
Kind
Vibes

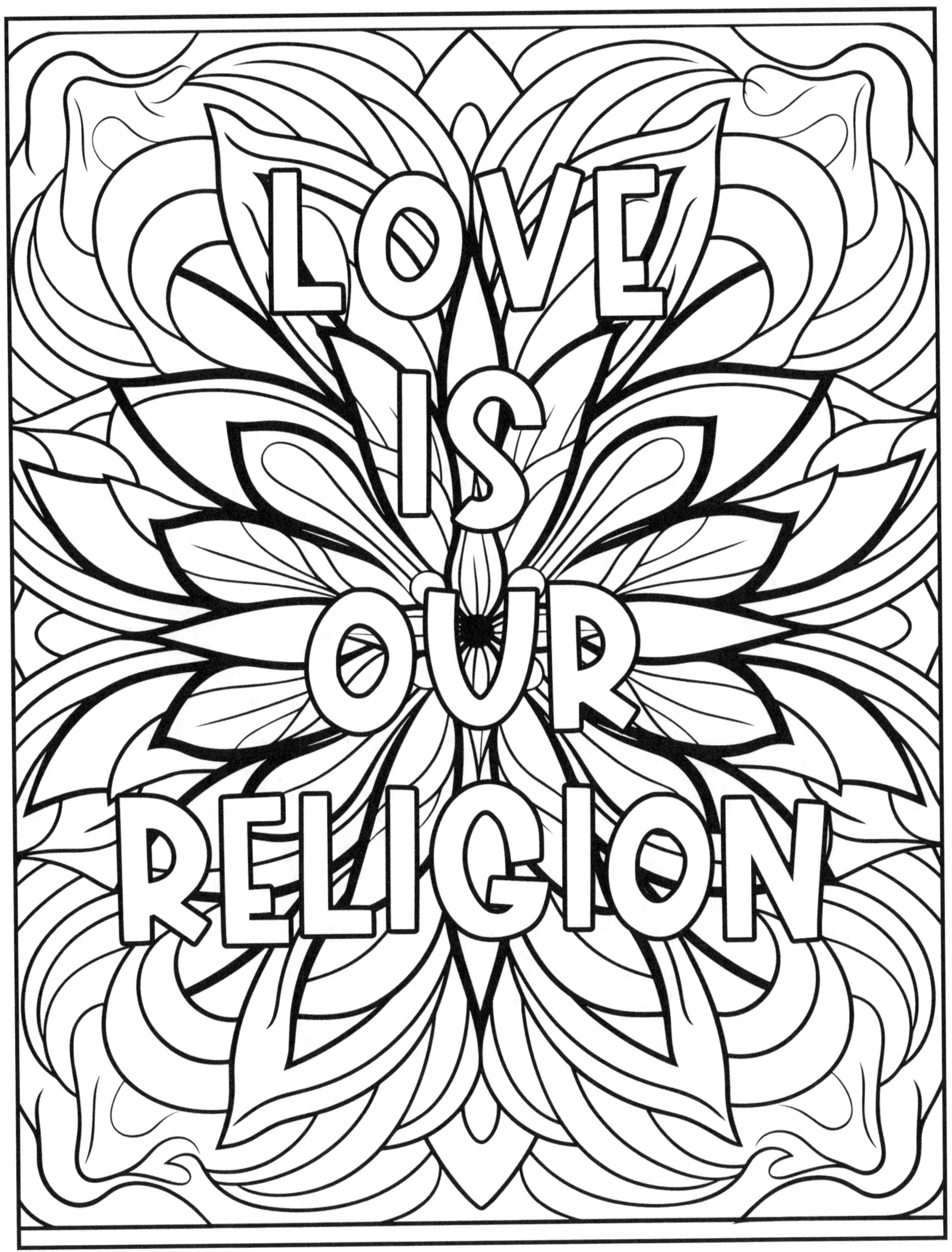

LOVE
IS
OUR
RELIGION

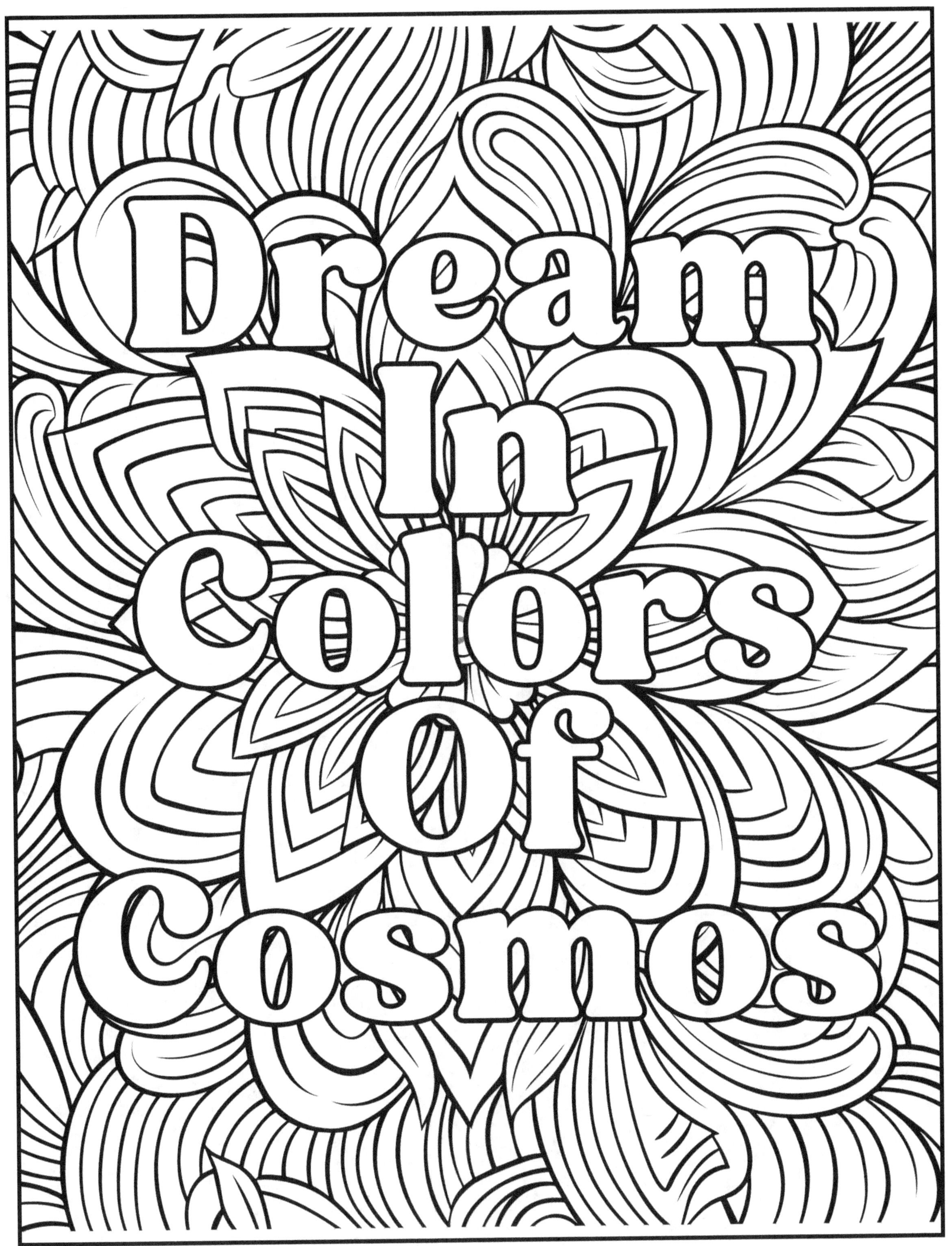

Dreams In Colors Of Cosmos

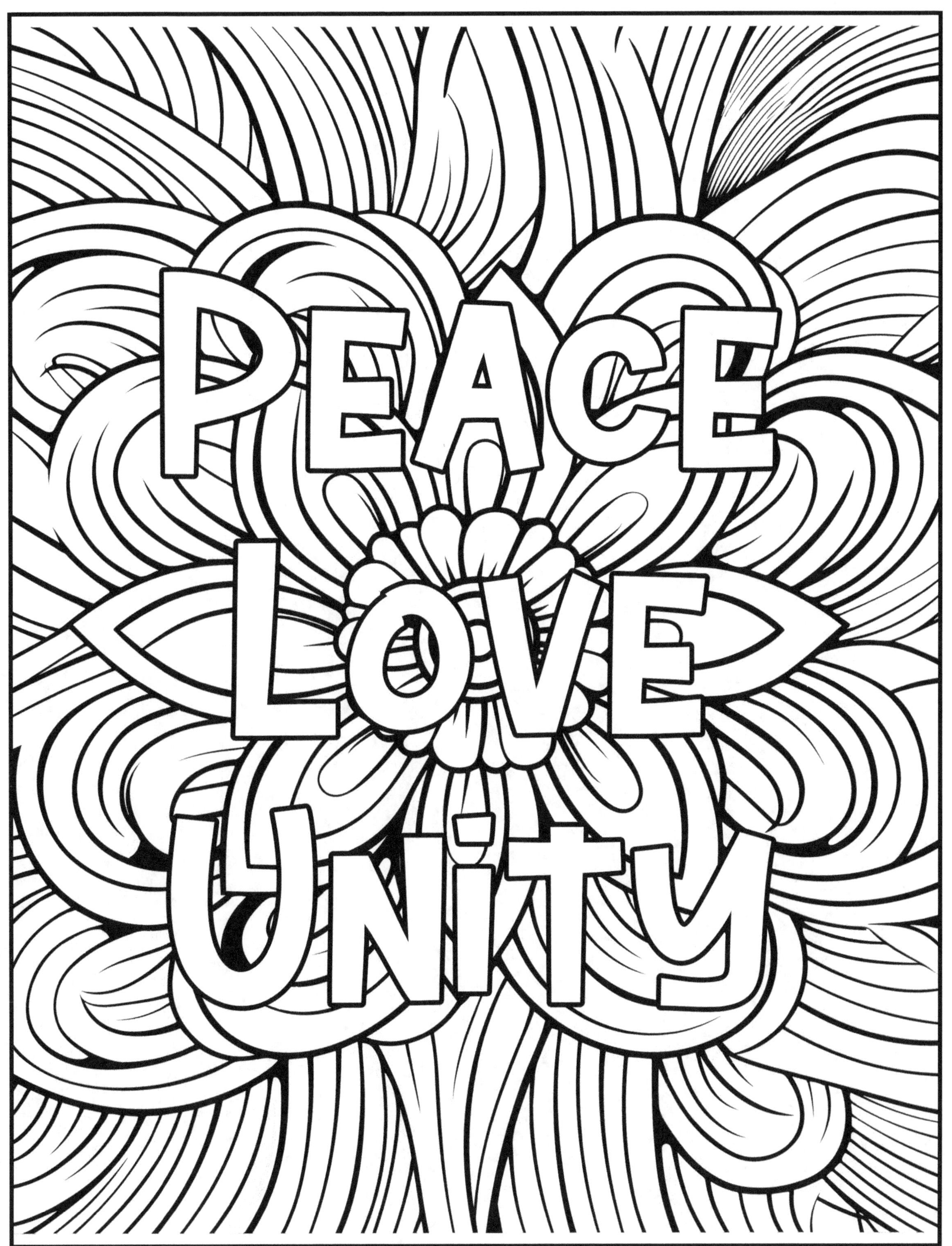

PEACE
LOVE
UNITY

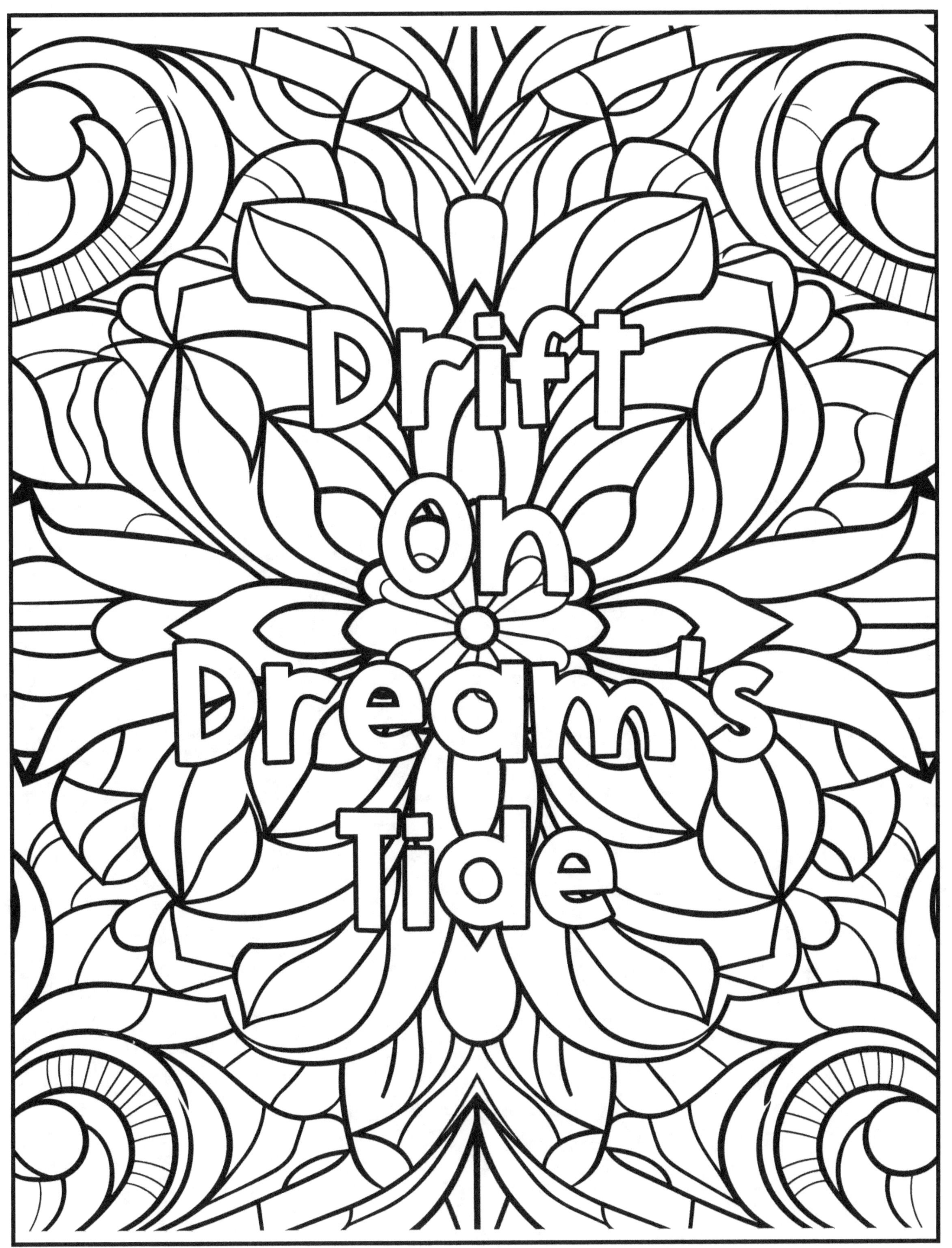
Drift
On
Dream's
Tide

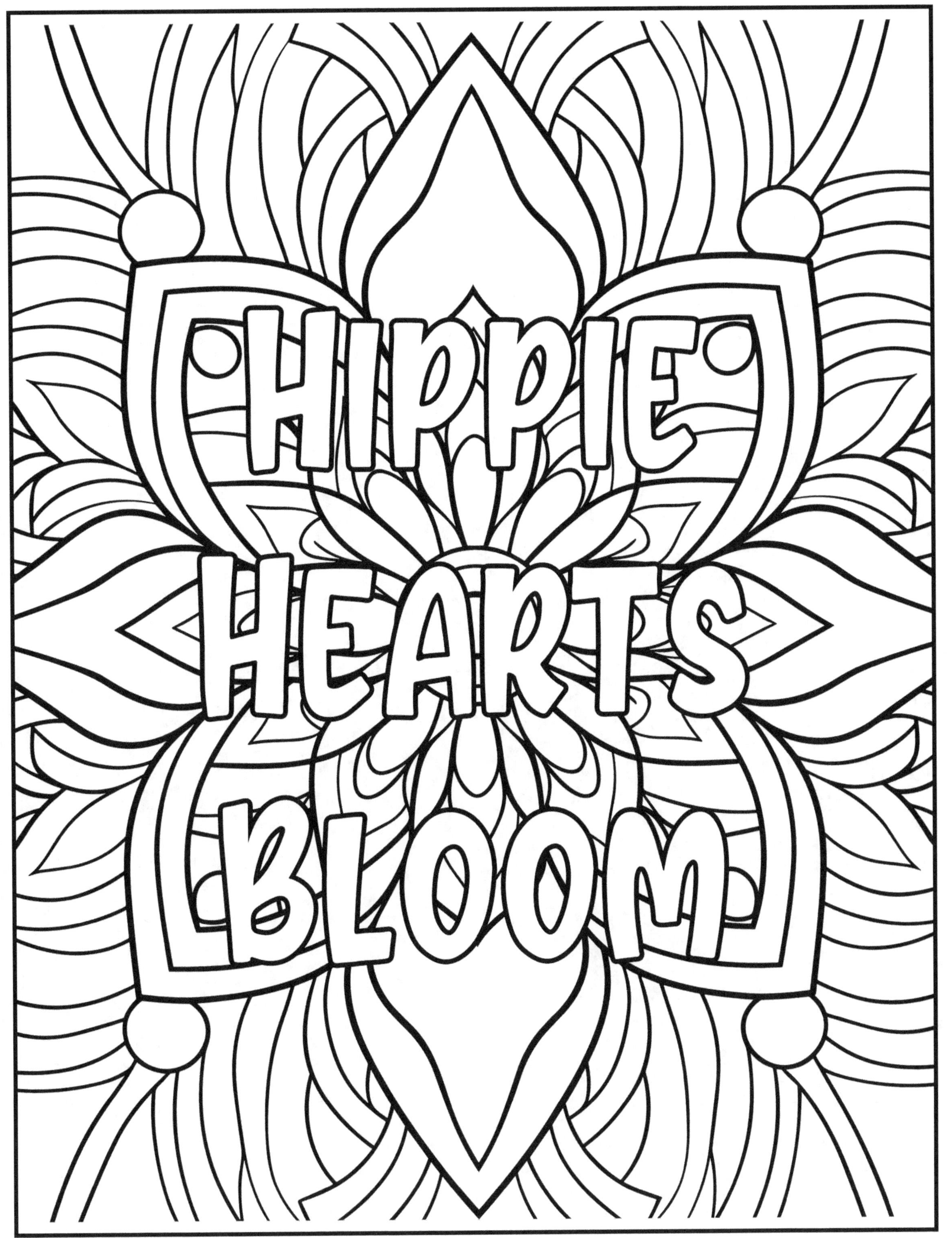

HIPPIE
HEARTS
BLOOM

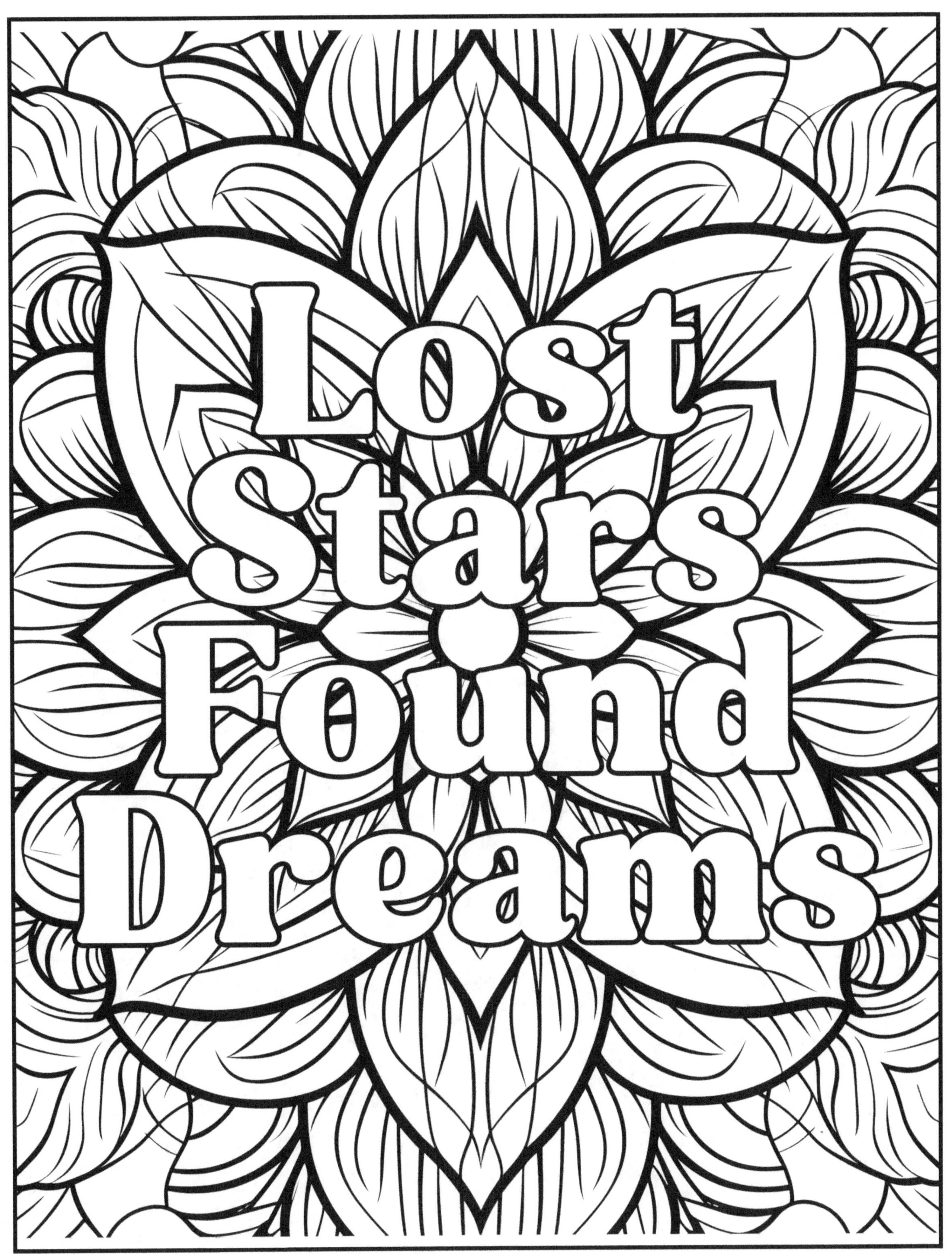

Lost
Stars
Found
Dreams

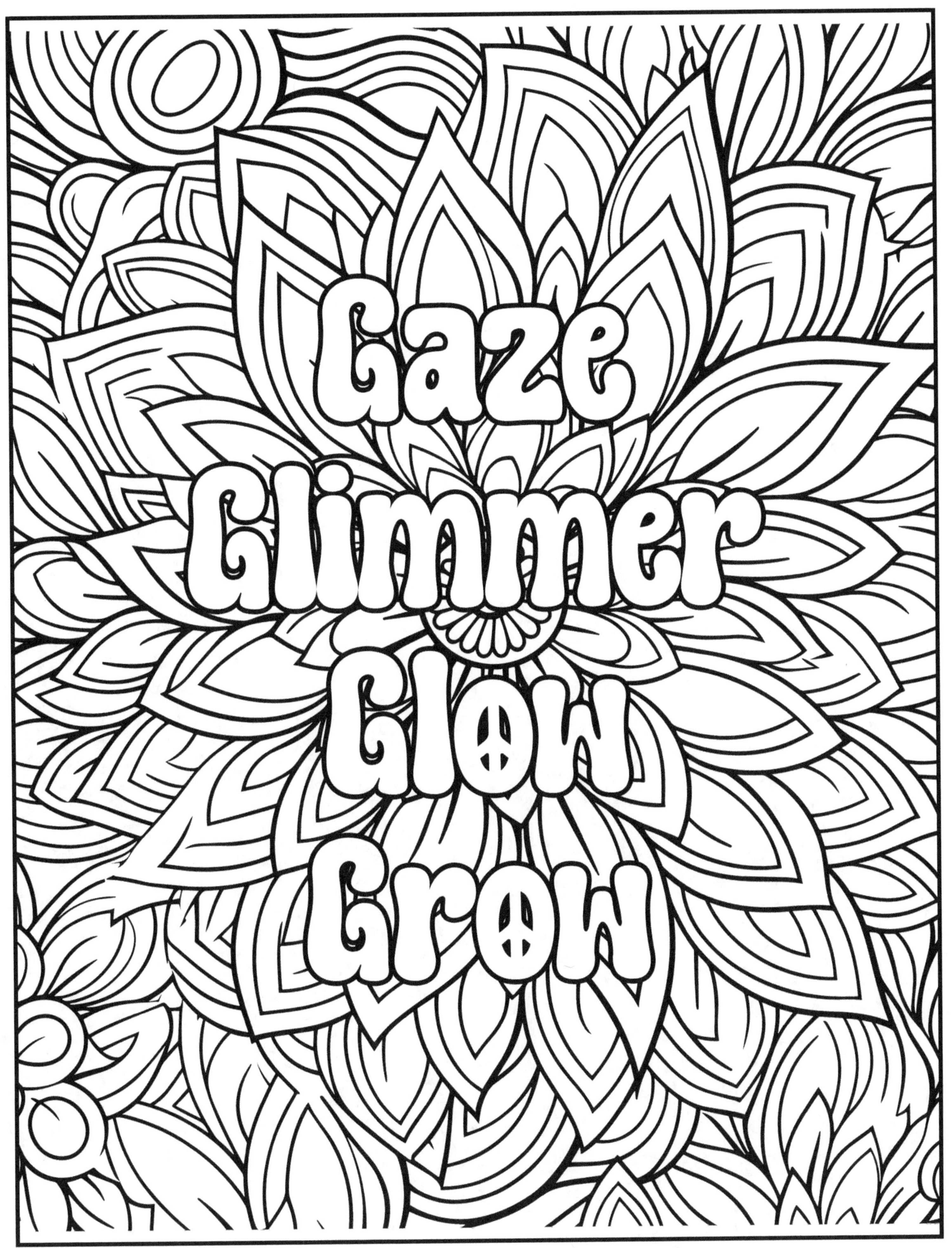
Gaze
Glimmer
Glow
Grow

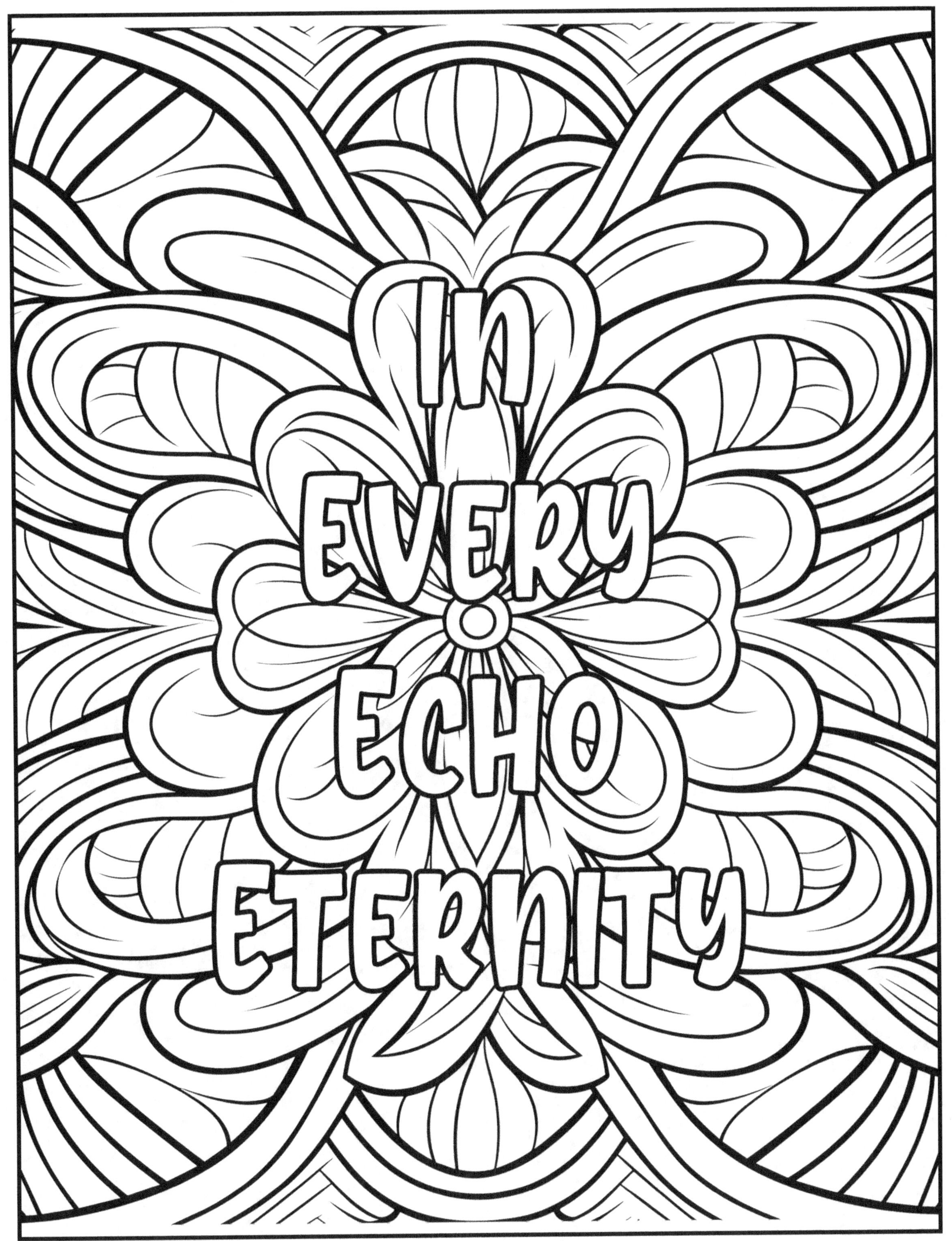

In
Every
Echo
Eternity

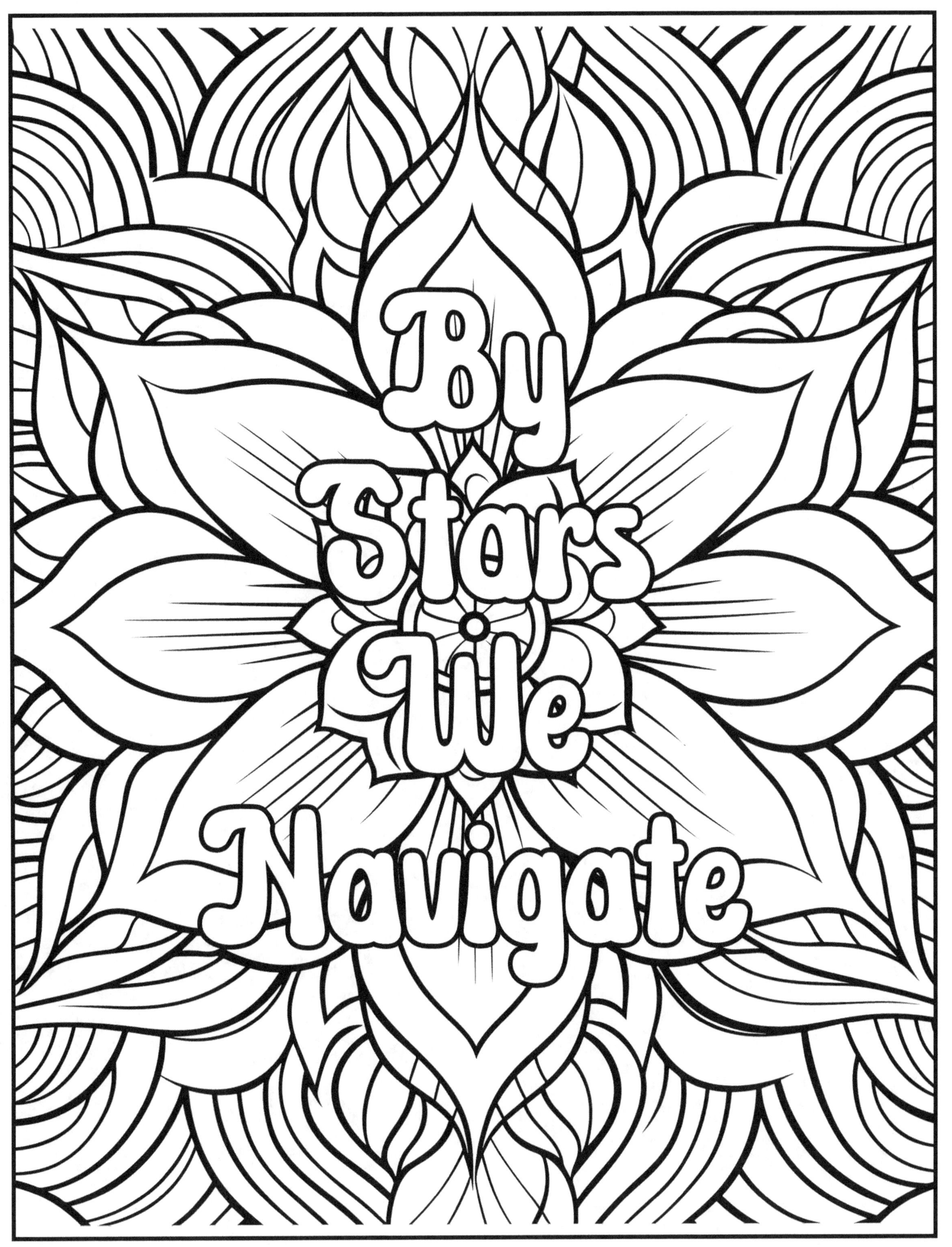
By
Stars
We
Navigate

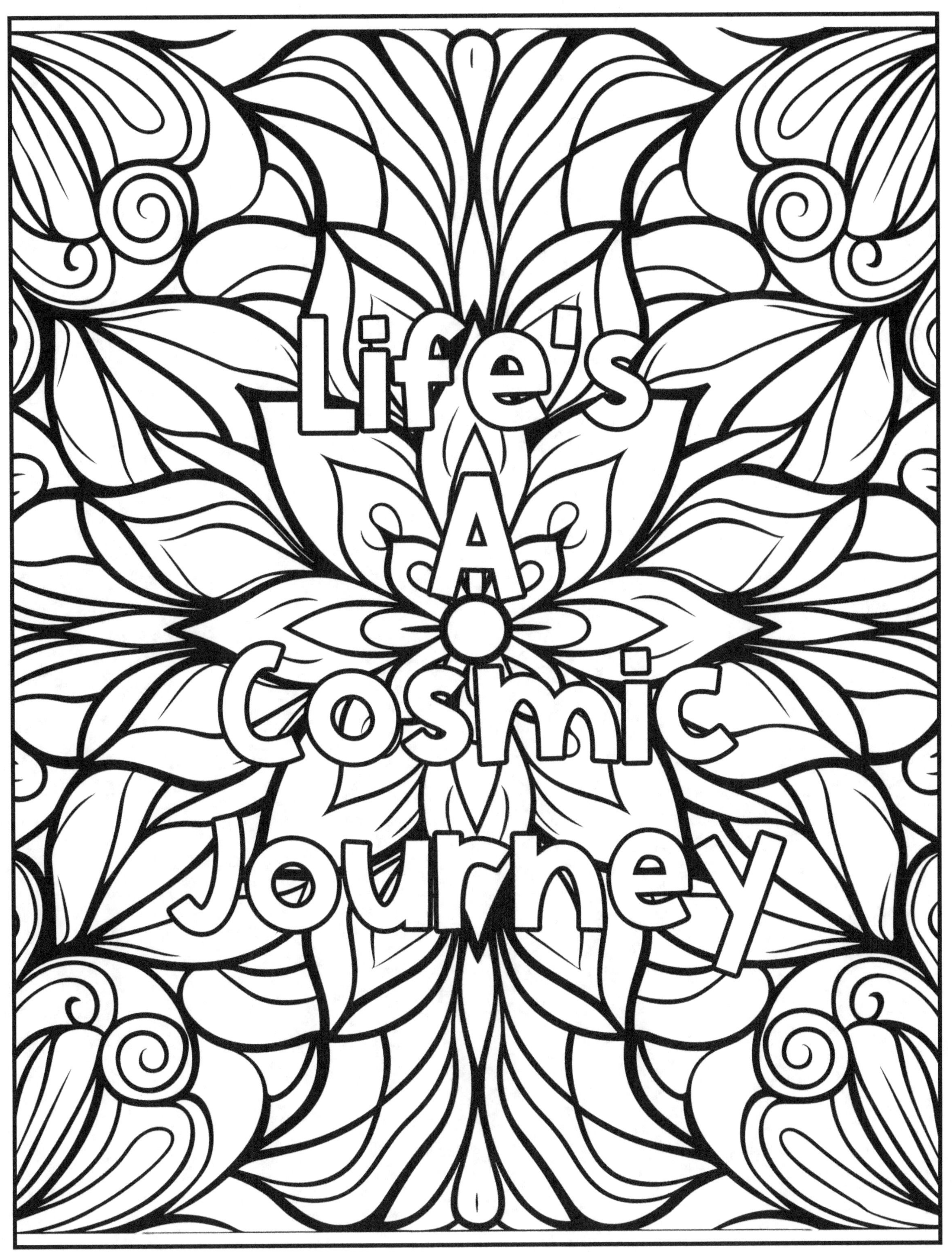

Life's
A
Cosmic
Journey

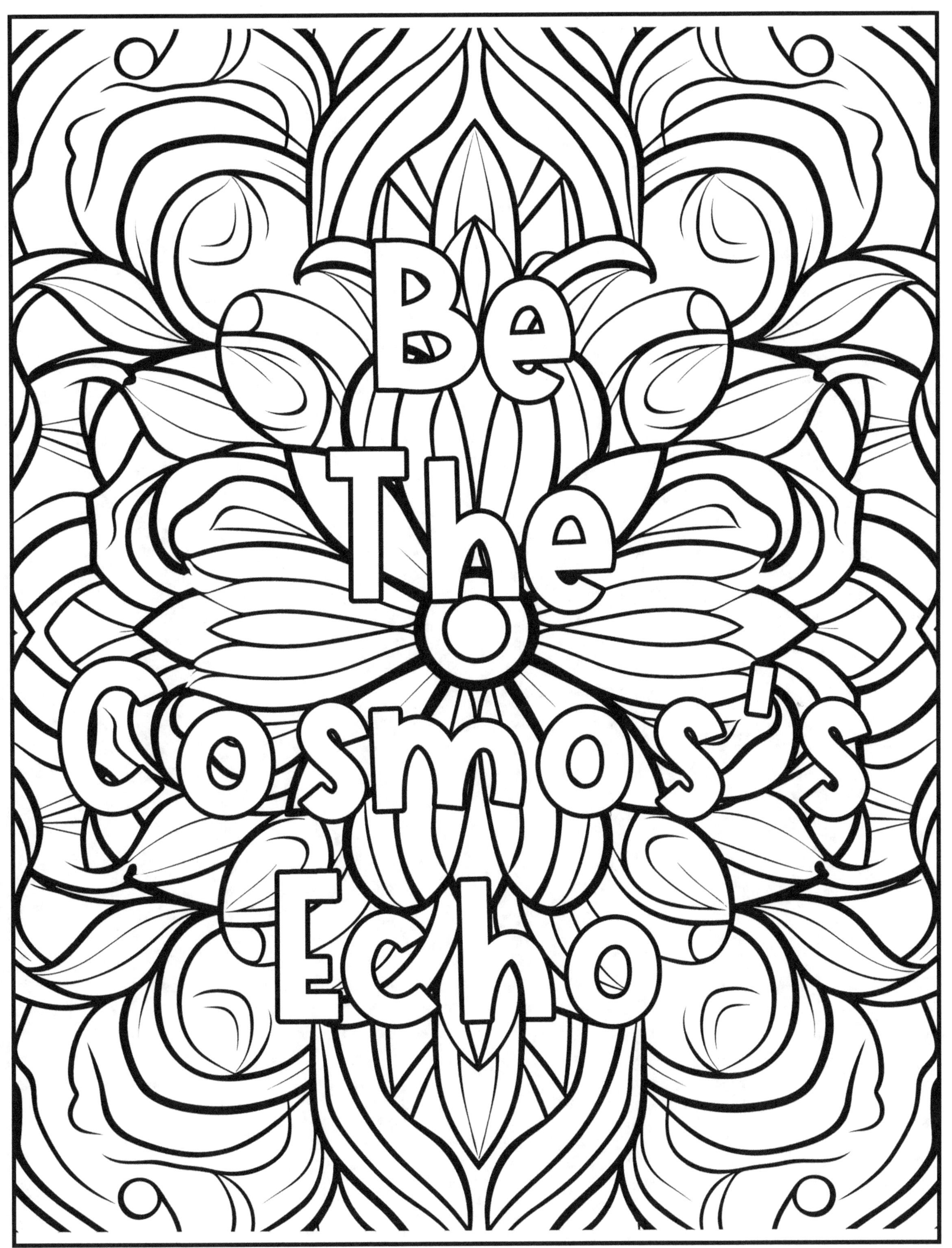
Be
The
Cosmos's
Echo

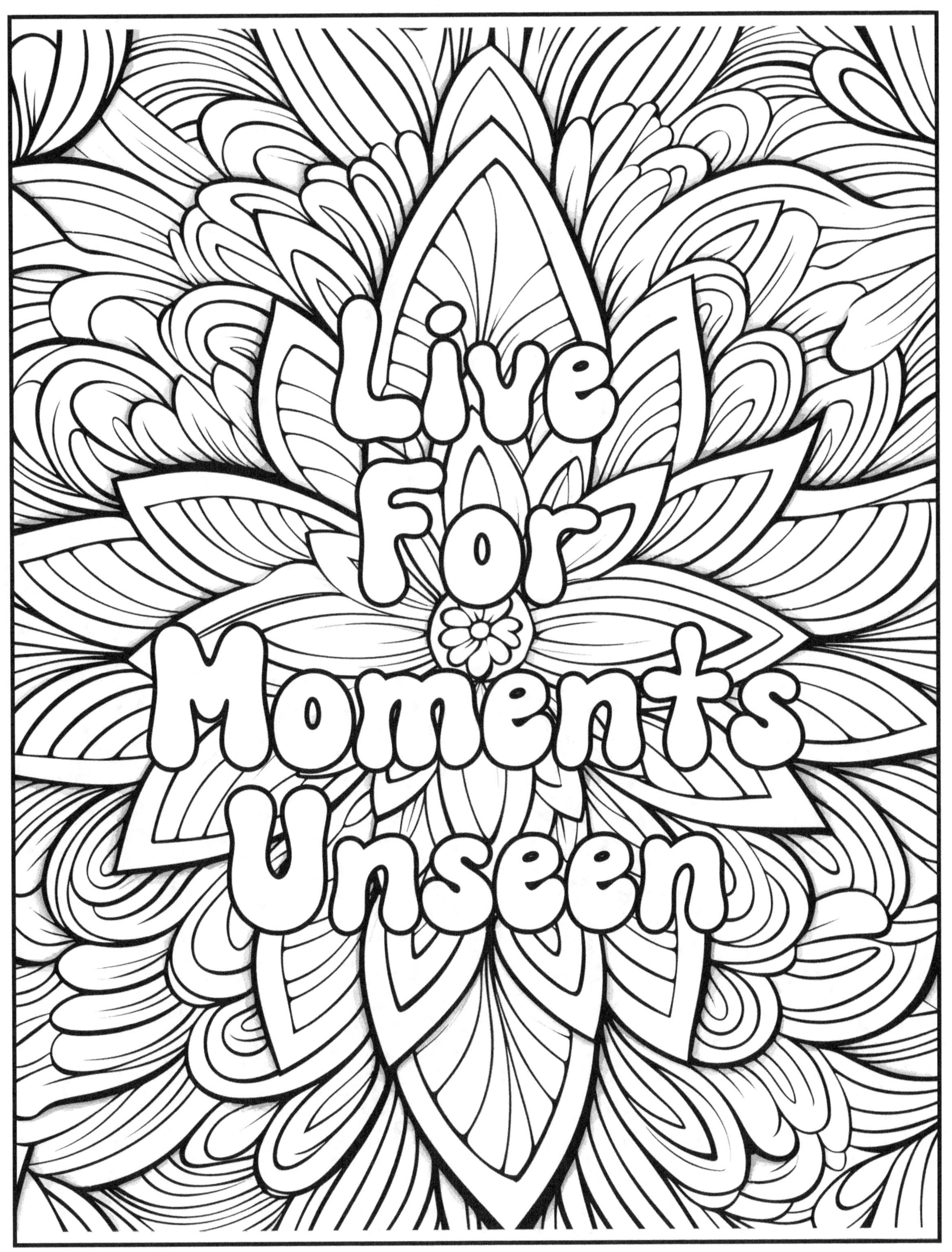

Live
For
Moments
Unseen

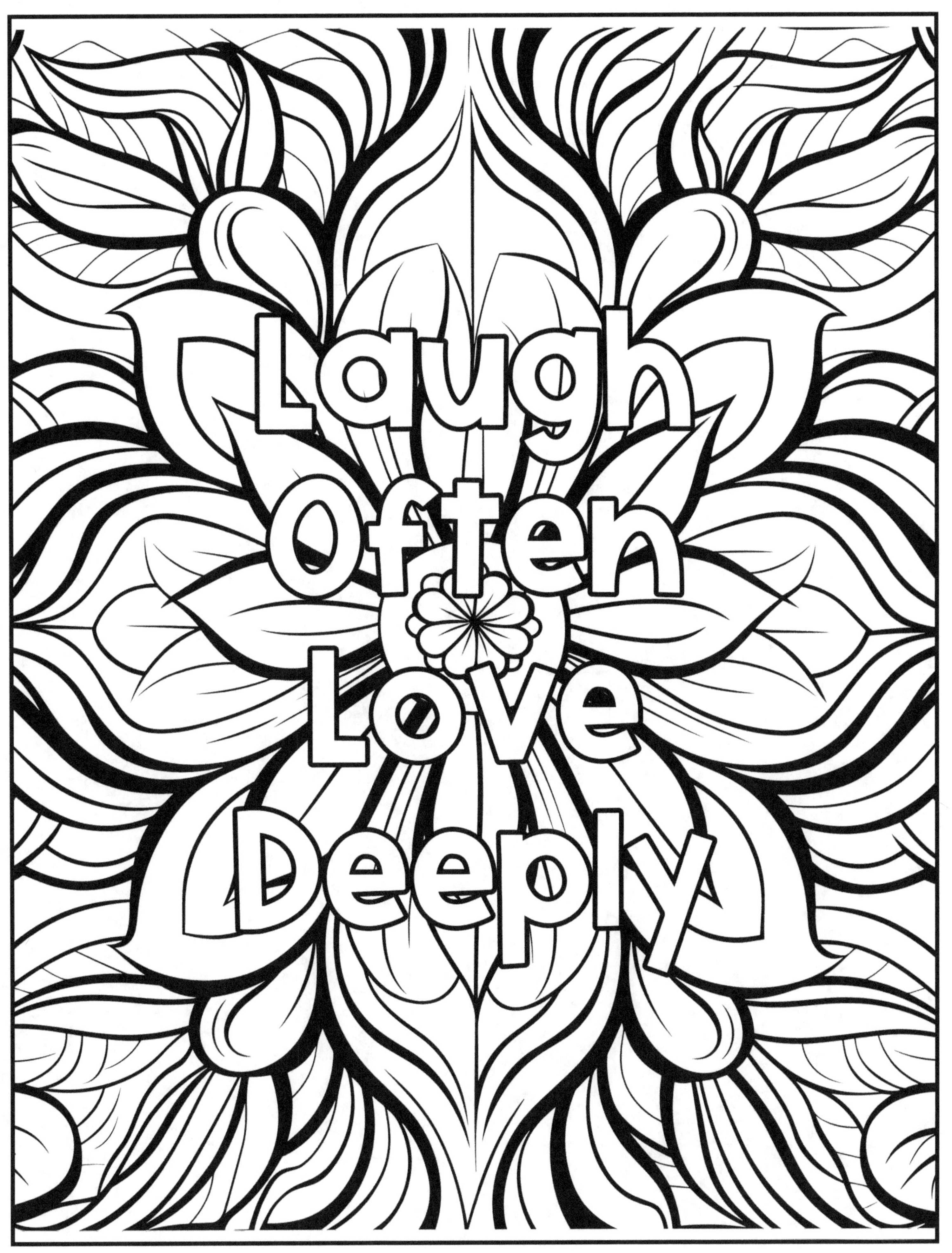

Laugh
Often
Love
Deeply

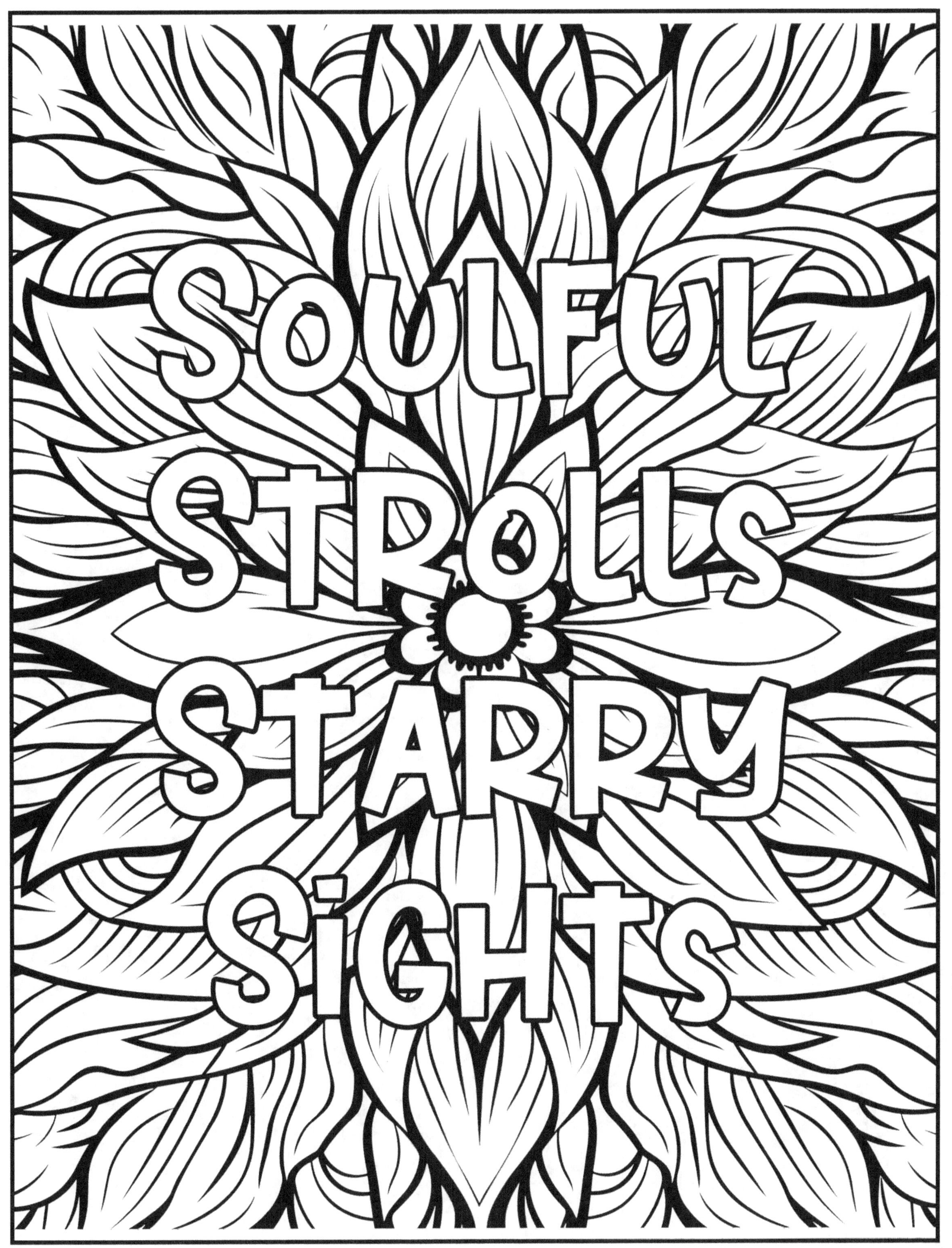

SOULFUL
STROLLS
STARRY
SIGHTS

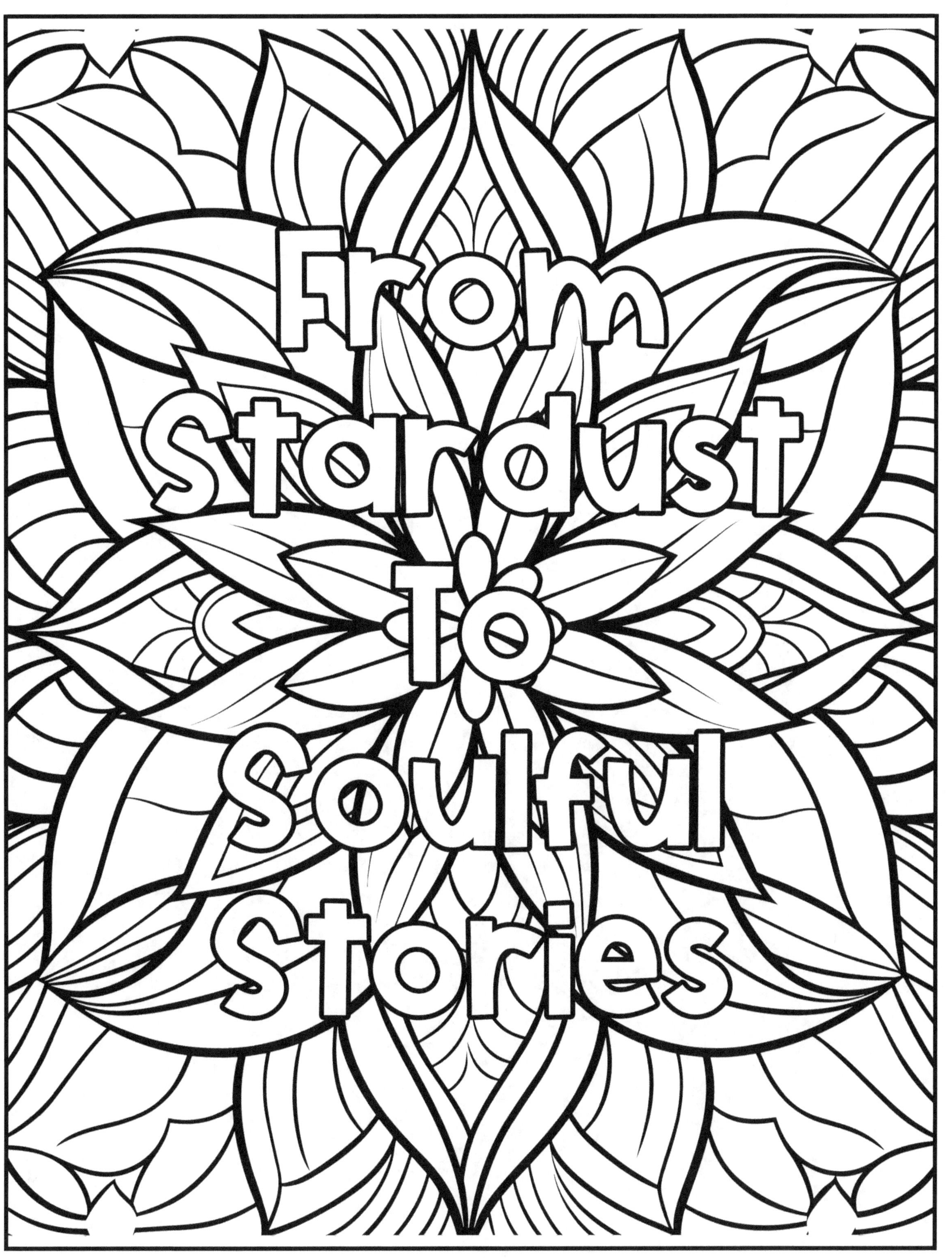

From
Stardust
To
Soulful
Stories

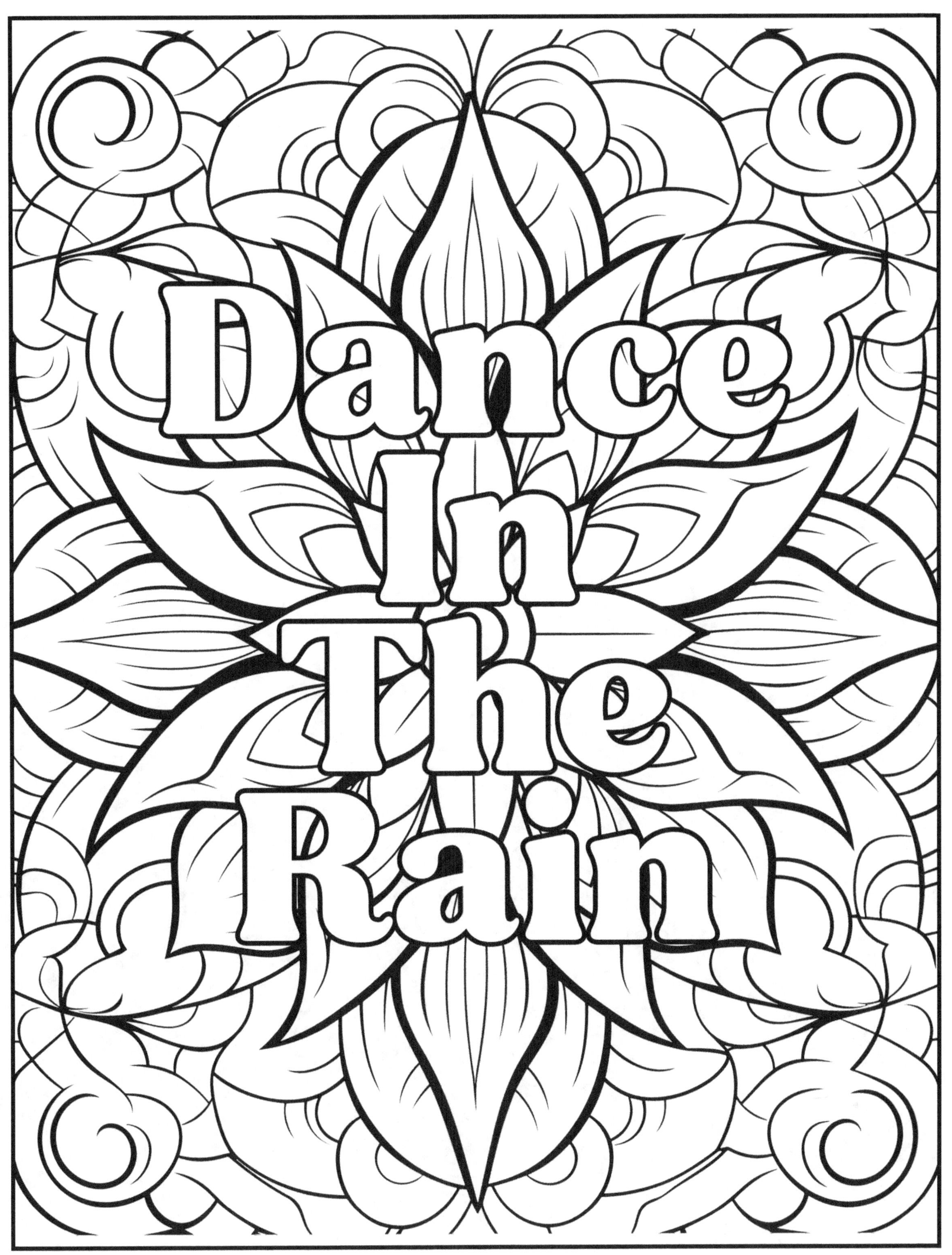

Dance In The Rain

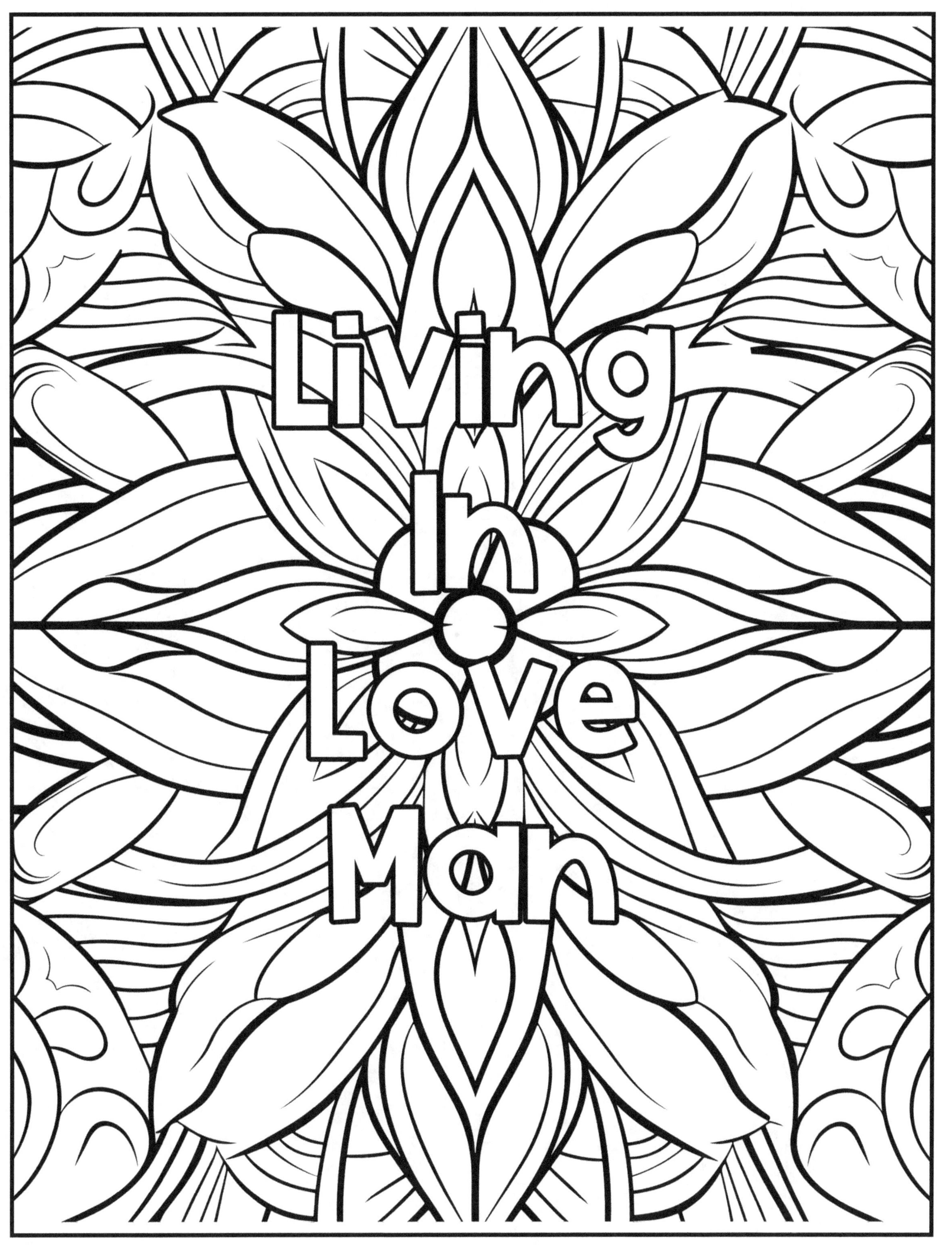
Living
In
Love
Man

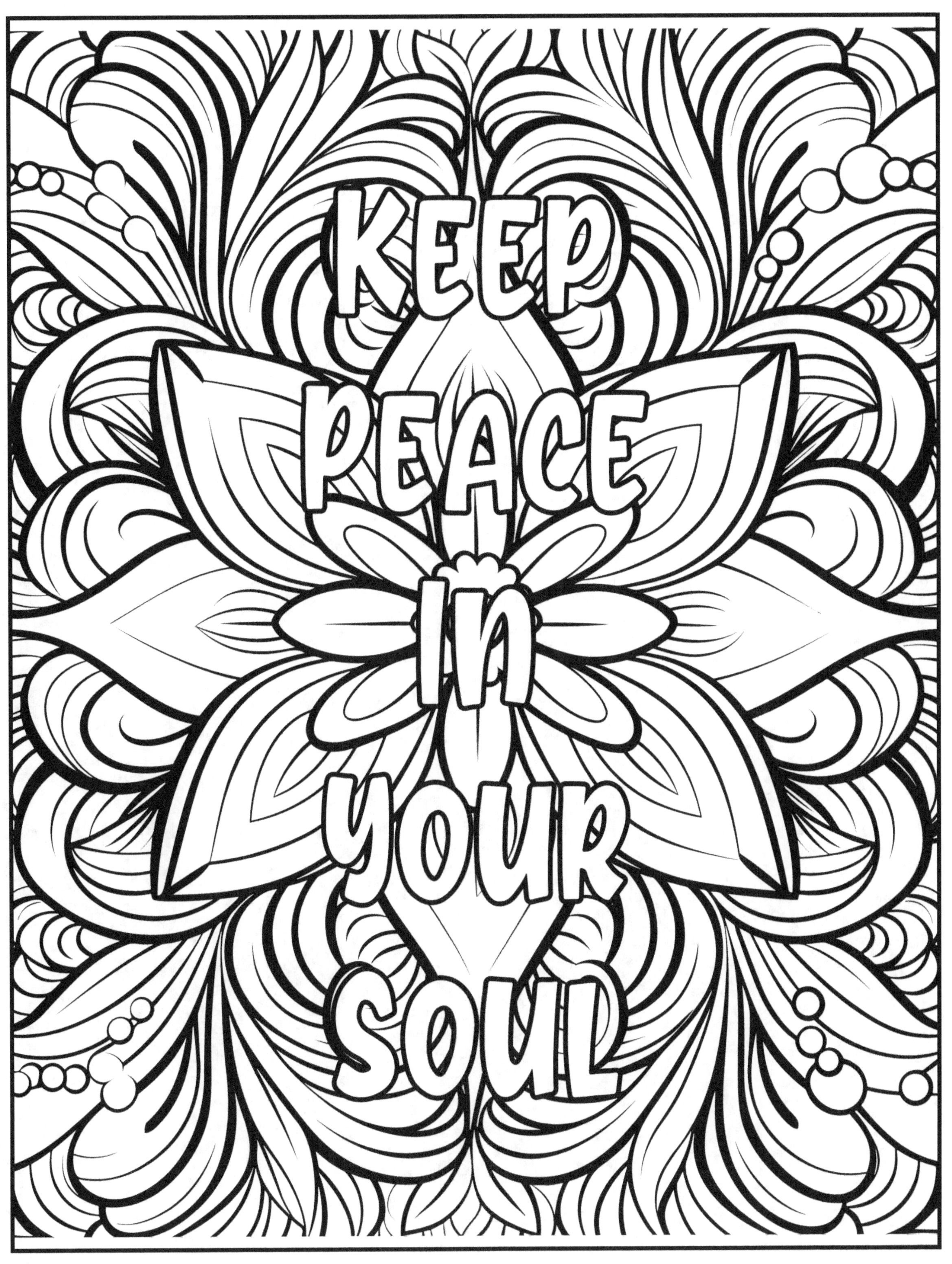

KEEP
PEACE
IN
YOUR
SOUL

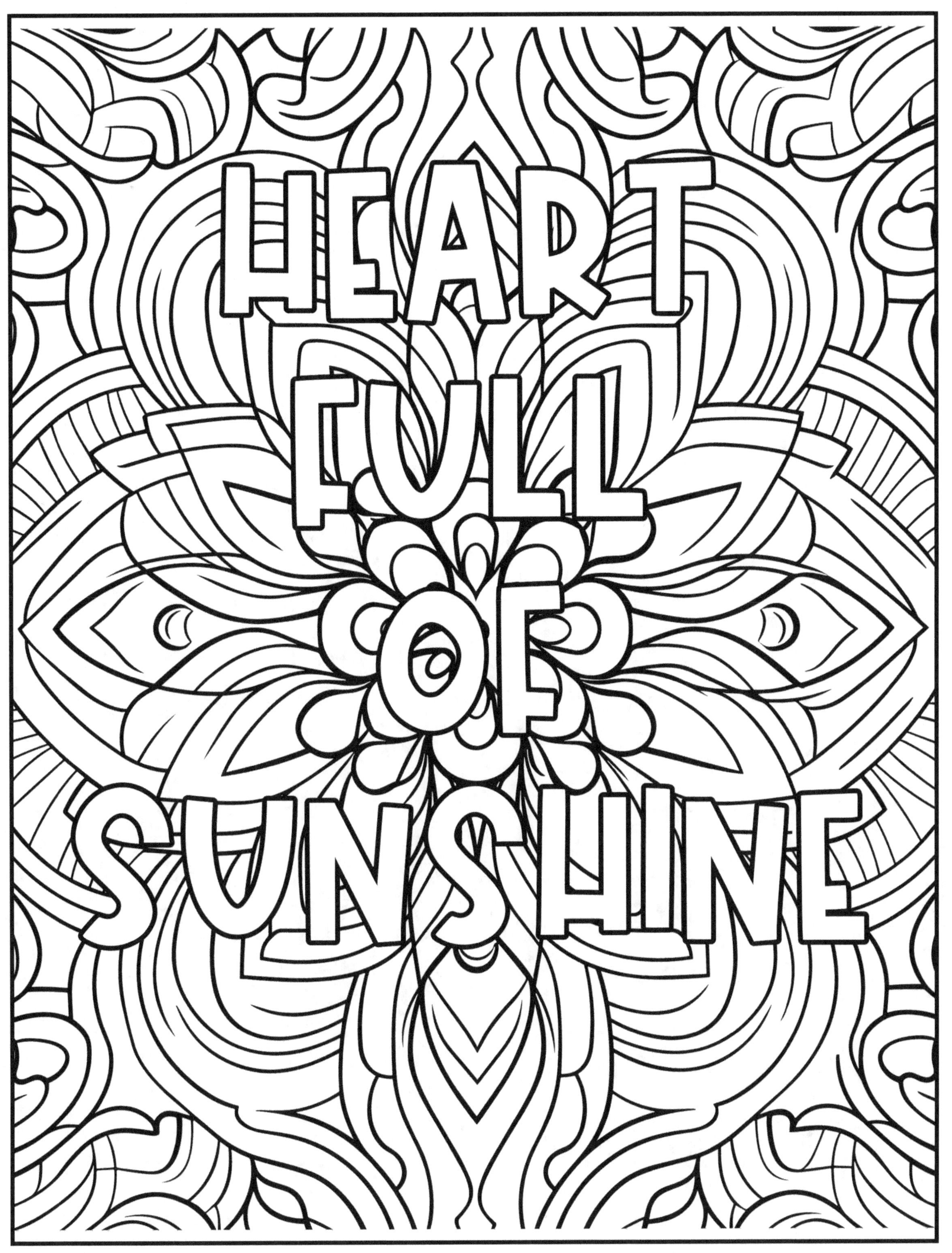

HEART
FULL
OF
SUNSHINE

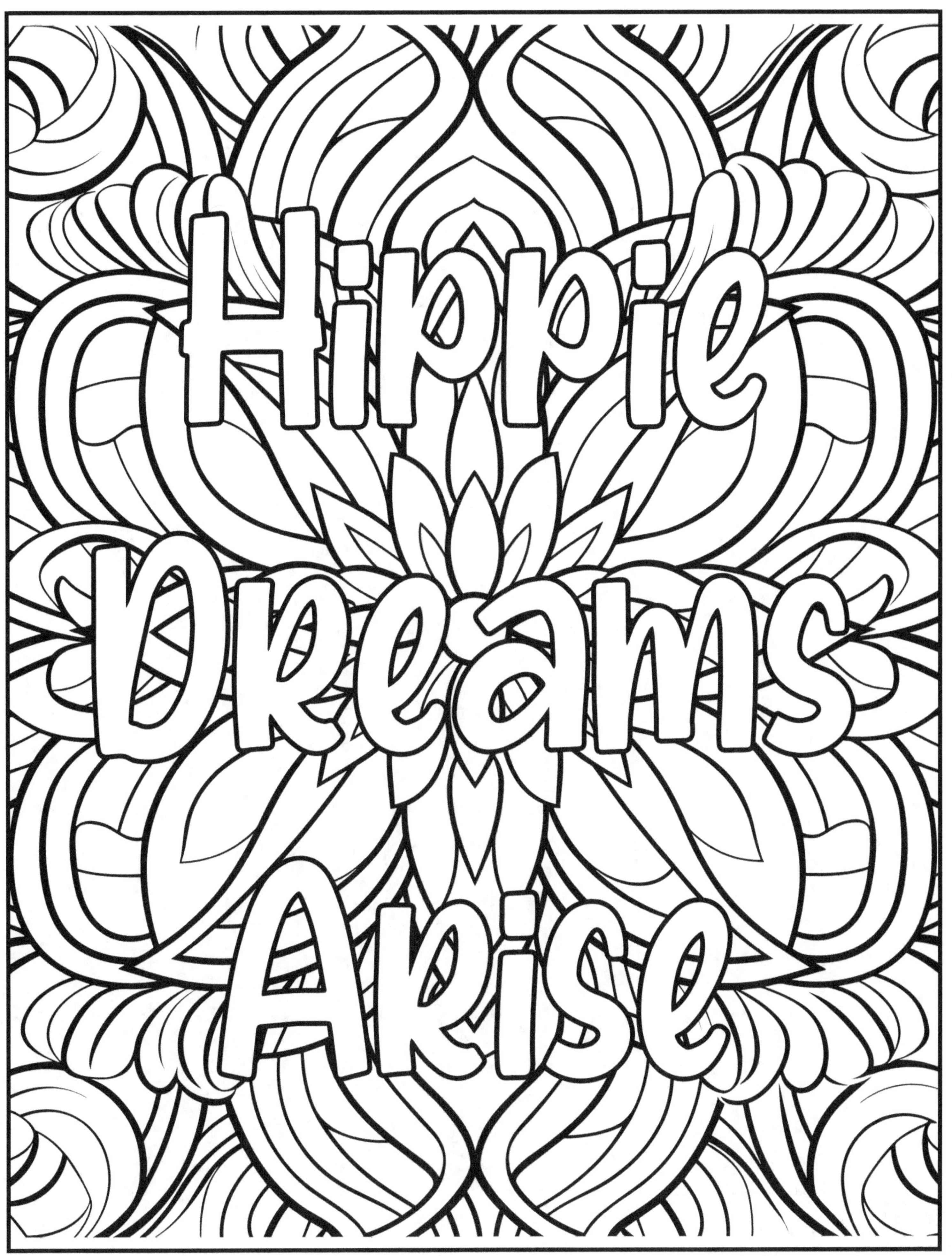

Hippie
Dreams
Arise